Group Games
&
Activity Leadership

Group Games
&
Activity Leadership

By Kenneth J. Bulik

Venture Publishing, Inc.
State College, Pennsylvania

Production Manager: Richard Yocum
Design, Layout, and Graphics: Diane K. Bierly
Manuscript Editing: Diane K. Bierly
Additional Editing: Deborah L. McRann and Richard Yocum
Cover Design and Illustration: Diane K. Bierly

Library of Congress Catalogue Card Number 00-100201
ISBN 1-892132-17-6

Contents

Forward

This book has been compiled over the years with an awareness for the need of a comprehensive reference for group games. The 500-plus activities in the following pages are intended to be used as a reference or a guide in the planning of larger group activities. Central themes have been established as foundations upon which to build more elaborately, either by adapting the given suggestions or branching off to make up a new activity. Some of the activities are new. Others may have been played in neighborhoods and playgrounds when we were children, or in parks by our parents and grandparents. Some activities may sound familiar, but have different names from what you remember. Few of these activities have established rules or strategies that must be followed. To the leaders of these activities: be flexible, and if necessary adapt the rules, conditions, and strategies of the given activities to meet the needs of your group.

This is primarily a book which has been designed to recall to the leader's mind familiar and not forgotten activities. The book is presented as a guide in which the old and new in group games will be easily understood and adapted to use in a variety of social and recreational settings.

Kenneth J. Bulik
Frostburg State University

Part 1
Activity Leadership

Activity Leadership

Methods for teaching and leading children through game activities vary according to the types of games used and the characteristics of the children. There are however, certain general methods of conducting group game activities. These are consistent with sound methods of education and leadership, differing only as they are applied to a specific type of activity. Methods of teaching and leadership for young children are built upon basic guides for selecting and presenting activities to children. These methods include selection of appropriate activities, cultural influences, the leader's preparation for presenting activities, the presentation of activity materials to a group, the organization of children into group and game formations, and the supervision of children during the activity.

Basic Principles

Activities for the school-aged child should provide opportunities for:

1. Participation in vigorous, gross motor activity, directed towards normal development of age-appropriate motor skills.
2. Achievement in the acquisition of activity skills and the elementary skills necessary for their participation, suitable for the age and ability of the participant.
3. Recreation through a successful experience of play with others.
4. Acquisition of a variety of activity, recreation, and leisure skills for life-long use.
5. Development of the social skills essential for group activity involvement including, but not limited to cooperation, fair play, willingness to follow rules, sportsmanship, and teamwork.

6. Experiences which challenge newly developed motor, social, and cognitive abilities through graded activities which build upon prior successful experiences.

Selection of Activities

The child's interest, age, needs, and abilities, as well as previous experience, availability, and adequacy of facilities, and the time allotted for the activity are the significant factors to be considered in the selection of an appropriate activity. It is recognized that interests are closely related to abilities as well as to a sense of competency in performance. It is also noted that ability includes not only the physical, but the integration of the social and cognitive domains as well. It is the leader's responsibility to determine and consider the age of the participants as well as their interests, needs, and abilities within their particular group, to be aware of facility and equipment needs and time allotment. The leader then selects activities reflective of these factors.

General activity characteristics for children in the primary (ages 6–8), middle (9–11), and upper (12–14) grades are summarized here. These activity characteristics may be applied not only to the specific age groups identified, but to the age group above and below the listed age group. The variability of needs and abilities increases with age. Therefore, these characteristics should be viewed only as guidelines. The leader's knowledge of the participants' needs and abilities should refine these guidelines.

Activities suitable for children in the *primary grades* require short periods of high-energy physical activity, as well as those of lower energy physical activity following a high-energy activity. Always allow for a wind-down activity after a high-energy activity. The circle formation, and the line formation are often used for introducing the activity chosen. Characteristics of activities for this age group include simple neuromuscular skills such as running, stopping, starting, changing directions, hopping, and dodging, and the basic skills of kicking, throwing, and catching large, soft balls. Children of this age group require activities of minimal direction and rules. Teaching is at a minimum; however, guidance and support will be necessary. Verbal praise for individual achievement is often utilized and is primary over the achievement of the group, which should be secondary.

Children in the *middle grades* begin to show characteristics that are developed further in the following years. Activities for children in this age group include those demanding vigorous physical activity of short duration, and those more passive activities which allow time to rest after vigorous activity. Increasingly difficult neuromuscular coordination movements, especially for the hands and upper body are being attained. Competence in running, stopping, starting, changing directions, hopping, and dodging as well as the basic skills of kicking, throwing, and catching increases and develops noticeably during these years. Both individual and group accomplishments are meaningful. Low-level team games should be introduced early in this age group. Participating as a team member brings satisfaction not seen in the earlier years. Low-level team games imply simple rules and directions for participation with minimal need for strategy.

Interests of the children in the *upper grades* are primarily found in intergroup and intragroup activities. These activities, whether cooperative or competitive, are of increasingly complex neuromuscular movements. Active gross motor activities are of longer duration and require more complex rules than in previous years. Strategy is often a necessary component for success in these activities and the basic skills should have been mastered. Skills being developed include a higher degree of accuracy and control and increases in speed, endurance, strength, balance, and agility. More complex neuromotor skills involving hand-eye and hand-foot coordination also develop noticeably. Skills required for various sports are often developed in simple team games such as base running, batting, catching, fielding, basketball shooting, passing, serving, and volleying. The leader takes on an additional role requiring not only the teaching of skills and strategy development, but of sportsmanship and teamwork.

Qualities of agility, balance, endurance, rhythm, speed, and strength are all requisites of coordinated physical activity. The acquisition of these qualities is a process beginning early in life and develops through participation in activities throughout the elementary years. The selection of activities for each age group and the procedures used in leading children in activities should allow opportunities for the development of these qualities progressively according to the maturity of the child.

Within almost every group, the leader will likely be able to identify various skill levels, especially as children mature. Using a bell-shaped curve concept, there are likely to be several participants whose skills are significantly above-average, and several whose skills are significantly below-average. The majority of participants will demonstrate average skill. Even within this group, the leader will identify several slightly above-average and several slightly below-average skills. Knowing the range of skills within the group, which specific subgroup does the leader target and select an activity for? In the bell-shaped curve, the few significantly above-average skilled participants can be referred to as *Group A*. These participants may demonstrate skills two or more standard deviations above the mean. *Group B* are part of the slightly above-average skills group, one standard deviation above the mean. *Group C* are slightly below average in skills and may be described as one standard deviation below the mean. *Group D* participants have significantly below-average skills and are two or more standard deviations below the mean. The leader will obviously program the session to target the most average skills group since an overwhelming majority will be from that group. However, the leader should specifically target the slightly below-average group (Group C) when selecting the most appropriate activity. If the leader targets Group A, with the selection of activities, they (Group A) will have their skills challenged. Group B participants may be able to keep up somewhat with some difficulty. Group C will have significant difficulty and Group D will be unable to participate. A significant number of participants will struggle and not benefit from the activity and those especially in Group D will take a further "hit" on their self-esteem. If the leader targets Group D, then that group will be able to participate appropriately for its skill level. Group C will do well in that activity, but Groups B and A will likely be bored and not benefit. Targeting Group B will have the same effect on Group D as targeting Group A did. Targeting Group C is most appropriate when selecting activities. All will be able to participate at a level which promotes success and fun. Members of Group A (whose self-esteem is already high), may take on the role of coach or official, if necessary. The primary goals in the selection of any activity are enjoyment, skill enhancement, and improved self-esteem. The leader should program activities which allow all members to participate free from unnecessary embarrassment and/or ridicule.

Cultural Influences

The effects of cultural and societal influences on activities has changed over the past several decades. For example, American society no longer accepts the notion that certain sports such as basketball and baseball are the domain of males or individual sports are the domain of white suburbia or team sports are the domain of the inner city. However, the leader's ability to demonstrate the sensitivity and awareness of an individual's culture may impact the session, the group, and the choice of activities. Even the leader's leadership style is now part of the total equation leading to a successful activity experience for participants. There have been many fine articles written recently detailing the beliefs and values of various cultures and subcultures, such as European Americans, African Americans, Asian Americans, Native Americans, and other groups based on religion, socioeconomic status, gender, residence in suburbia or the inner city, age, and even membership in single-parent families, all of which may impact activities and activity leadership. Each culture or subculture will view a situation based upon common experiences, beliefs, values, education, and language, and interpret these situations through its *cultural filter.* The value placed upon competition versus cooperative play, expressive forms of activities versus physical play, and strong female leadership versus male-dominant leadership, may hold one meaning for the leader, another meaning for some participants, and even other meanings for the rest of the participants. The activity leader, being aware of these personal cultural filters seeks to provide a variety of experiences, meaningful to all members of the group, rather than expecting the participants to adapt to what the leader holds meaningful. A successful leader will be able to be a positive role model not only by being fair and friendly, or by demonstrating competence as a leader or in activity skills, but also by demonstrating interpersonal skills respectful of, and sensitive to, the belief and value systems of the group.

Preparation

Beyond the selection of an appropriate activity, the leader's preparation for presenting the activity includes providing a safe environment, adequate facilities, and time allotment. The leader must know the activity thoroughly before attempting to present it to the group; have all equipment (including backup equipment) ready for use; have boundaries set up; have adequate support staff if needed to act as umpires and referees; be aware of any potential safety hazards and remedy these hazards prior to the start of play; and have a plan of *how* to present the activity. It must also be noted that part of the preparation time includes planning alternative activities should the original plan not be fully implemented (e.g., time remains after original activity is completed, inclement weather, unsatisfactory response from participants, and skill level of participants). Alternate activities should be limited to activities somewhat similar in nature to the original activity to avoid wasting time in changing activity location (inside versus outside or gym versus a multipurpose room), the need for different materials and equipment (Frisbees versus craft materials) and the need for detailed instruction for the alternative activity. This is by no means a suggestion to limit variation of the alternative activity, but just a suggestion to the leader to keep in mind the response of the participant if too much time is taken up in the transition, especially if unplanned. A smooth, well-planned transition is always the goal when changing activities.

Presentation

Of significant importance is the manner in which the leader presents the chosen activity to the participants. Different approaches may need to be used based on the ages of the participant, whether the activity is familiar or novel to the participant, the location where the activity will take place, new skills needed for participation, and the number of participants involved in the activity. It is not the intent of this book to detail each presentation approach. There are, however, several general procedures common to all approaches:

1. Initially, the group should be organized into the activity formation appropriate for the activity (see Activity Formations).
2. The leader will introduce himself or herself if he or she is new to this group or if new participants are joining the group.
3. The leader will state the name of the activity and the general nature of the game (e.g., tag, ball, team).
4. The explanation on how the activity is played, scored, and ends should be as clear, concise, and brief as the age group can tolerate.
5. Especially with younger participants, the leader will ask them if anyone has ever played this activity before. If some have played before, the leader will ask them to share with the group how the activity is played and several of the rules needed for participation.
6. Once the directions of the activity are completed, the leader will give the participants an opportunity to ask questions.
7. In order for the leader to be sure that the participants understood the directions for the activity, he or she will ask several movement questions of participants to determine their level of understanding. This is especially important with the younger participants.
8. In some cases, a demonstration or a practice game may be needed for greater understanding of how the activity should be played and what is expected from the participants.
9. The leader will begin the activity. The leader should let the activity take its course; however, if a teachable moment presents itself, he or she should take advantage of the moment. Additional rules and strategies can be added the next time the activity is presented, or if the activity begins to break down, and/or the participants are struggling with their ability to complete the activity in an enjoyable manner.
10. After the activity is concluded, the leader should bring the group into a circle or line formation to process and receive feedback. Did you like this activity? What made it enjoyable or not enjoyable? How could the activity be improved or changed next time? This time is important for the participants to give the leader their feedback and ask questions. It is also an opportunity for the participants to wind down and for the leader to reemphasize the purpose of the activity and group as well as to make any announcements.
11. Last, but of utmost importance, the leader will make sure that positive verbal feedback and praise is given either individually and/or to the group as a whole for their positive participation. Verbal praise should *not* be limited to the end of the activity, but throughout the activity. Such positive reinforcement from the leader is especially meaningful and goes a long way in developing a positive rapport with the group.

Presentation of an activity is also not limited simply to the nuts and bolts of teaching and leading the activity, but occurs before, during, and after the activity. The way the leader "sells" the activity beforehand, seeks the involvement of those not certain if they want to participate, the motivation and enthusiasm for the activity itself, for the group, and for the individual members of the group, should all be considered part of the presentation. There are many fine activity leadership textbooks available which address the various roles and tasks of the activity leader and should be read and referred to often.

Group Formations

Many of the group games listed in this text require breaking the large group of participants into smaller units. The leader's ability to accomplish this quickly and easily contributes to the success of the activity session. Breaking the group down into teams or smaller groups can be done several ways. Like most techniques, there will be an advantage and a disadvantage to each. It is up to the leader to choose which techniques are most appropriate for his or her group. It is however, advisable to use a variety of techniques. The following are several of these techniques.

Leader-Directed

This technique is very structured: the leader assigns each participant to a specific group or team. The advantages to using this technique include faster transition from presentation to activity participation, enhanced competitiveness and fun, promotion of social integration, and encouragement of assumption of different roles. The leader, knowing the skills of the group, can ensure skill equity among the various groups which will enhance the competitiveness and fun of the activity. Enhanced competitiveness will promote social integration of the groups, instead of cliques sticking together, and will enable the participants to learn to assume different roles within the group. The disadvantage to this technique is the structure itself. Especially with older participants, the structure may diminish the excitement of the activity. Participants may feel more comfortable assuming traditional roles within their group and want to have control over their activity. As children mature, they typically seek independence from authority (the leader), seek autonomy within their group and demonstrate competency to themselves and their peers. The leader-directed technique is authoritarian in nature and may be counterproductive with some groups.

Peer-Directed

This technique uses participants as a leader, or captain, of their group or team. Taking turns, each captain chooses a member for his or her team. The advantage to this technique is the relinquishing of control from the leader to the partici-pants. The disadvantage to this technique is the public recognition of the skill level and social popularity of each group member. The child who is consis-tently the last to be picked will undoubtedly lose much needed self-confidence and self-esteem. To counter this possible effect, instead of choosing the high-est skilled participant to act as captains, the leader may choose lesser skilled participants. These lesser skilled participants will likely choose their friends first, letting the higher skilled participants wait their turn.

Random

This technique is often used in various formats such as counting off by twos and threes or dividing the group by whoever is wearing the color white or has brown hair. The goal here is the random selection. Occasionally there may be a significant skill inequity among teams, and the leader may need to make some adjustments to ensure fair play and fun for all.

These three mentioned techniques all have several formats each. It is up to the individual leader to choose which technique is best suited for the group. The leader should keep in mind that there is no one best technique for all situations; rather, he or she should use a variety of these techniques to ensure fun for all.

Activity Formations

As stated previously, the group should be organized into the appropriate for-mation for the activity. In many cases, the activity formations described here should be used for the presentation of the activity. At other times, one forma-tion may best be used to explain the fundamentals of the activity, and then the participants may be organized into the proper activity formation.

Line Formation

This formation has each participant lining up to stand or sit side-by-side on a designated line facing the leader. This is a generic formation to the beginning of almost any activity session. It may be best to have younger children sit on the line rather than stand. This may keep distractions associated with standing and fidgeting to a minimum, thereby allowing the children to focus better on the instructions of the activity leader. This formation is considered more for-mal and structured than some of the others. The advantage to this formation, beyond the structure, is that all participants can see the leader. The leader's back is never to the participants. The disadvantage to this formation occurs if there is a relatively large number of participants. If the line becomes too long, those on either end may have difficulty hearing the instructions. This can be remedied by making two parallel lines. Another potential disadvantage to this formation as part of the activity presentation may occur if a gross motor movement is used as practice before the activity is begun, such as practicing or reviewing Simon Says or the Hokey-Pokey or even a forehand tennis stroke. In these cases the participant may have difficulty visualizing the movements and then performing the movements. While the leader may demonstrate the movement to be performed once or twice, he or she will usually work the line and give individual attention, leaving the others to wait their turn. In this case, a circle formation may be preferred because each participant can see others perform the expected movements and will better be able to copy what they see. In other cases, a line formation may be best, as in practicing an overhead tennis serve with the use of a tennis ball. Common sense should win out in determining when to use a line or circle formation.

Line formations are also often used to begin a specific activity such as Angels and Devils; Steal the Bacon; Red Light, Green Light; and Make Me Laugh. Usually with older children the leader may begin the activity presentation in these line formations natural to the activity itself. In many of these activities, two or more lines are made, facing each other, but some distance apart. The leader should stand off to one side, equidistant from both lines. This will enable the majority of players on both lines to see and hear the leader. The leader must be aware of the acoustics of the facility and other distracting background noises which may prevent the participants from clearly hearing the leader's instructions. The leader should make every effort to speak clearly and loudly enough for all to hear. In an effort to overcome these natural background noises, the leader should lower the pitch of his or her voice, increase his or her tone, and slow the rate of the words he or she is speaking.

Circle Formation

This is also a simple and quick formation and can be used when meeting a group for the first time. If possible, the leader should utilize lines already on the floor to form the circle (e.g., center of a basketball court). The circle formation makes for more of an intimate setup. Each person is the same distance away from the leader, as opposed to the line formation where some at the ends of the line may be quite a distance away from the leader. The circle formation allows for a more face-to-face interaction among the participants. If the group is especially large, the leader may use a two-deep circle. An additional advantage to this formation was described in the previous section. When practice activity movements are needed, the visual feedback from the other participants doing the same movement may be helpful. An obvious disadvantage to this formation is the leader will always have his or her back to some members of the group. In most cases, the leader stands in the middle of the circle and makes the presentation. The leader should slowly keep rotating around so no one person only sees his or her back. If the leader stands outside the circle, those on the far side of the circle may have difficulty seeing and hearing the leader. As with the line formation, the leader must make every effort that all members clearly hear and understand what is being said, even when his or her back is towards someone. Background noises should be less of a problem since the participants are closer to the leader.

Circle formations are often used to begin a specific activity such as Duck, Duck, Goose or Protect the King. The circle can be enlarged as needed after the leader's presentation has ended. The leader should move outside the circle for supervision. Depending on the activity itself as well as the ages of the participants, the leader may want to position himself or herself near those participants who may tend to be disruptive and in need of frequent cueing. The leader may also position himself or herself near someone who may need verbal praise or encouragement or physical assistance. In other cases, moving to different positions around the circle will enable the leader to observe the action from different angles and give verbal praise, feedback, and/or assistance to a greater number of participants.

File Formation

This formation is used for most relays. It is rarely used as part of the leader's presentation, unless the participants are familiar with the relay activity and need only minimal instruction. There are as many files as there are teams for the relay.

Team Formation

Team formations vary for different team games and sports. In many cases the leader will start the session with the participants in either a line or circle formation. After teams are chosen and the participants have found their formation for the game, the leader may review the goals of the game, and any other relevant information the participants may need. Basketball, baseball, football, and volleyball are all examples of team formations.

Free Formation

In free formation, the players begin the activity scattered about over a wide area. This formation is likely to be used with many games of tag. This formation is the most free and unstructured. The leader should be aware that free formation is likely to produce horseplay among the younger players. The leader would be wise to move quickly into the game itself with only the minimal instruction needed and time for organization.

Supervision

Supervising the activity itself requires the greatest amount of planning to ensure a safe environment, maintain enthusiasm for the activity, and ensure a sense of fair play. Improper supervision is a major cause of injury. Therefore, certain guidelines for proper supervision should be established and followed. Guidelines may vary depending on the age and characteristics of the participants, the location of the activity (e.g., beach versus gymnasium), and the activity itself (e.g., a ropes course versus Duck, Duck, Goose).

Supervision Suggestions

Suggestions to leaders for proper supervision of a group:

1. *Always* maintain visual contact with participants.
2. *Never* turn your back on the group. If a participant comes to you to ask a question, place the participant in front of you, so the group is still within your visual field.
3. Know how many participants there are in your group (especially in an outdoor setting) and make frequent head counts.
4. Ensure a proper participant-to-leader ratio. It is impossible for one person to properly supervise a large group. Depending on the age of participants, the activity, and the location, perhaps a 20:1 ratio for most activities and a 10:1 ratio for aquatic activities (1:1 ratio for aquatic activities where there is a child with a history of a seizure disorder) is best.
5. Use only properly trained leaders for higher risk activities, e.g., aquatics, ropes, gymnastics, horses, and archery.
6. Maintain equipment in proper working order. Use equipment only as it was intended to be used. This includes a system for general maintenance and inspection of equipment.
7. Make sure the activity area is free from hazards. This also should include a system for general inspection of the area.
8. Consideration for age differences, size differences, and skill differences is important, especially in activities where physical contact is likely.
9. Develop the spirit of fair play, follow the rules, and instill a healthy sense of competition.
10. Stop the activity if horseplay occurs. Remind the group of your expectations and possible consequences for continued horseplay. Resume the activity when cooperation is achieved.
11. Never attempt to explain anything until quiet and attention is absolute.
12. Make sure that all understand the rules and expectations of the activity. Allow participants to make some rules governing play (when appropriate).

13. If an activity is going poorly, stop the activity and iron out the difficulty.
14. Know the activity well before implementing the activity. Be confident in your officiating and decisions.
15. Most games can be modified to meet the equipment and space available.
16. Introducing slight variations may help in maintaining interest and enthusiasm.
17. In team games where individuals intermingle, mark one team well so that the players are easily identified.
18. Use nonverbal techniques to stop unacceptable behaviors when appropriate, before using verbal techniques:

   a. ignore minor behavior infractions;
   b. use facial gestures to indicate displeasure (e.g., nod of the head or frown);
   c. use physical proximity to those involved in minor horseplay;
   d. use light physical touch (e.g., pat on the shoulder or back) to show awareness of horseplay;
   e. use a verbal reminder for those involved (e.g., reminder of expectation or consequences); and
   f. use verbal redirection (e.g., giving of consequences).

19. Give frequent verbal and nonverbal feedback to individuals and group for positive and/or improved behaviors and skills.
20. Know when to join in the activity and when not to:

   a. *Do not join in* when close supervision is required, e.g., issues of safety are raised, larger group, impulsive participants, skills observation is necessary.
   b. *Do join in* when close and direct supervision is either not necessary or can be attained even while participating. Joining in the activity not only is fun, but can lead to improved rapport between the leader and the participants. When you do join in, participate at the level of least competency. This should not be your forum to show off or to boost your ego!

Part 2
Group Games

Games for the Primary Grades

Angels and Devils

The players are divided into two teams. One team is called the *angels* and the other group is called the *devils* (or any other team name of choice). Goal lines are established and clearly marked at both ends of the activity area. The angels are standing on one goal line and the devils are standing on the other facing each other. The angels are instructed to turn around so their backs are to the devils. The leader then silently instructs the devils to sneak up on the angels. When the devils are around 10 feet or so away (or any reasonable distance) from the angels, the leader will yell out, "The devils are coming." This is the signal for the angels to turn around and give chase to the devils who then are running back to the safety of their goal line. Any devil who is tagged by an angel before reaching his goal line now becomes an angel. This game is now repeated as the devils turn their backs and the angels sneak up on the devils.

Additional Comments:
- The activity area between goal lines can vary depending upon the age of the participants. Thirty to forty feet apart is recommended.
- As an alternative to joining the opposite team, the tagged participant is eliminated from the game. The game continues until all members of one team have been tagged. This alternative may not be appropriate for the youngest participants; however, for older participants, the team competition may add to the excitement of the activity.
- The leader should encourage skill development in starting quickly, changing directions, running, and other gross motor movements. Listening skills, following direction, and good sportsmanship should also be encouraged with frequent verbal praise and excitement from the leader.

- Depending on the equity of skills on each team, the leader may vary the distance or closeness one team is as it approaches the team with its backs turned before the leader calls, "The _____ are coming." The goal is to have a good chase.

Call Ball

The players are in a circle formation with one child in the center. He tosses the ball above his head while calling the name of a child in the circle. That child attempts to catch the ball before it bounces more than one time. If she catches the ball, she may take the place of the child in the center and toss the ball. However, if she fails to catch the ball, the child in the center continues to toss and call until a player is successful in catching the ball.

The game may be changed by penalizing the child when she does not catch the ball; that is, she must be the tosser if she fails to make a fair catch.

Additional Comments:
- The leader may use several small circles with about eight players in each circle.
- The leader may use a volleyball, playground ball, or a beachball.
- The leader should teach the children to call the names clearly so that all may hear and to call the name as they toss the ball.

Charlie Over the Water

The players are in a circle formation and hands are joined. One player is Charlie and he stands in the center of the circle. The players walk to the left (or right) around the circle chanting:

> Charlie over the water,
> Charlie over the sea,
> Charlie caught a blackbird
> But he can't catch me!

As they say, "Me," the players squat quickly. Charlie tries to tag a player before the player gets into a squatting position. If he is successful, the child whom he tagged changes places with him and the game is repeated with the new Charlie in the center.

Additional Comments:
- The leader may choose another player to help Charlie if he is slow in tagging someone.

- The leader should not let the game drag before someone is tagged. Two or three children may be Charlie at the same time if the group is large, in order to keep the game active and interesting.
- The leader should watch for fairness in tagging. A rule that hands must be placed on the floor or upon the child's knees to qualify as a full squat may facilitate decisions.
- The leader should change the direction of movement around the circle to avoid dizziness.
- For a variation, the safety position can be changed or the group may skip to the rhythm of the chant.

Jump the Creek

Two lines are drawn to represent the banks of a creek. The children run and jump over the creek. Anyone missing the jump and landing in the creek is sent "home" to put on dry shoes and socks; he goes "home" and pretends to take off and put on his shoes and socks, and then reenters the game. The small child enjoys dramatizing this procedure, and it does not keep him out of the game because he missed a jump.

Additional Comments:
- The leader should keep the game informal when the group is small. If the group is large, or if the game is played in the classroom, the children should get into a file and wait their turns.
- The leader may use this game to develop courage in jumping and to teach different types of jumps: take off and land on both feet, leap from one foot to the other, leap across after a run, and so on.

Variations:
- The leader may vary the width of the creek or make a bridge to cross the creek—this may be a line and the children cross over with heel-to-toe steps.
- The leader may indicate stepping stones to bring in variations in leaping and taking long steps.

Dog and Bone

One child is selected to be the dog. She sits on a chair or stool in front of the children who are sitting in chairs. The dog closes her eyes. Her back is toward the other players. The dog's bone which is a blackboard eraser, or any article of similar size, is placed near her chair. A child selected by the activity leader attempts to sneak up to the dog and touch her bone without the dog's hearing him. If the dog hears someone coming, she turns around and says, "Bow! Wow!"

Then, the player must return to his own seat. A child who is successful in touching the bone before the dog hears him becomes the dog and the game is repeated.

Additional Comments:
- The leader should indicate the child selected to touch the dog's bone by beckoning or by nodding. The selection should be made quietly.
- The leader may appeal to fair play to maintain absolute quiet during the game. The children will be quiet as they learn that it is more fun if everyone keeps very still.
- The leader should allow waits of unequal length between attempts. This will keep the dog alert. If she turns when no one has left his seat, the dog should give her place to another child.

Drop the Handkerchief

The players stand in a circle formation facing the center of the circle. One child is IT and he runs around the circle and drops a handkerchief in back of and close to another player. He continues to run around the circle, and the player behind whom the handkerchief was dropped picks it up and runs in the direction opposite to that taken by IT. The player who first reaches the vacant place in the circle is safe and the other player is IT. The child who is IT takes, or keeps, the handkerchief and the game is repeated.

Additional Comments:
- The game may be played with a beanbag or knotted towel in place of a handkerchief.
- The leader may divide a large group into small circles of about eight players.
- The leader should not allow the children to play the game for a long period of time because it allows activity for only a few children to participate at one time.
- The leader should guard against the selection of favorites and encourage the children to drop the handkerchief behind a child who has not played.

Variations:
- This game may be changed into a tag game. The player who picks up the handkerchief chases the player who dropped it. The runner is safe upon reaching the vacant place in the circle. If he is tagged before he reaches safety, he is IT again.

Frog in the Sea

A circle about six feet in diameter is drawn on the floor or scratched on the playground surface. The child selected to be the frog sits cross-legged in the center of the circle. The other players chant:

> Frog in the sea . . .
> Can't catch me!

They step in and out of his circle, touch him, and dare him to catch them. The frog tries to tag someone without leaving his sitting position. Anyone whom he tags changes places with him and the game continues. The frog must not leave his sitting position. If he does not keep this position while tagging a player, the tagging is unfair and the child who was tagged does not change places with the frog.

Additional Comments:
- A large group may be divided into play units of six to eight players each with their own frog, or two or three frogs may be used in a larger circle of nine to fifteen players.
- The leader should teach the players courage and the frog cunning by encouraging the players to venture close to the frog. The frog must learn to surprise the players in order to tag them.

Huntsman

One child is selected to be the hunter. She stands in front of the group and says, "Who wants to go hunting with me?" Those who want to go on the hunt say, "I do!" Then, they get in place in a file behind the hunter. As soon as those who are going hunting are in place the hunter leads them anywhere within a designated play area. They must follow her and do everything that she does. Suddenly she calls, "Bang." This is the signal for all the players to run back to their seats. The player who is back in his own seat first will be the next hunter.

Additional Comments:
- The leader should be prepared to suggest follow-the-leader stunts suitable for his or her group and the room in which the game is played. The first-grade child may do such stunts as skipping, hopping, walking on all fours, going around chairs, and touching objects. These may be hunting-related stunts such as sneaking up on the prey, carrying a gun, and sighting targets.

I Saw

The players are seated in a circle. One child is in the center of the circle. He says, "On my way to school (church, my friend's house, or whatever), I saw _____." He then imitates in movements or gestures what he saw and the others try to guess what is was. The child who guesses correctly goes into the center and the game starts over again.

If no one guesses correctly, the child in the center tells what it was he saw. If his imitation was good, he is praised and allowed to be IT again. If the imitation was poor, he joins the circle and another player is selected to show what he saw on the way to school.

Additional Comments:
- The leader should tell the children that they must raise their hands and be called upon for their guesses. This eliminates confusion.
- The leader should praise a child's good attempts to imitate. Imitations will occur quickly if the first player is successful. The leader may need to suggest things which can be imitated, such as a dog, pony, automobile, cat, bird, airplane, and postman.

Shark and Minnow Tag

Two goals are set about 50 feet apart, with a "cave" on one side near midfield. Minnows stand at each goal, while the shark lurks in the cave. When the minnows run to change goals, the shark tags as many as he can. Minnows tagged become sharks and must join hands, with the original shark always at one end and the first minnow caught at the other end of the line. These are the only two sharks that can tag. If the minnows can break the line none can be tagged until the line is re-formed. The last one caught is the shark for the new game.

Who's the Leader?

A circle is formed. IT goes out of the room and one of the children in the circle is named the leader. When the children begin clapping, IT comes in, and the leader changes motions, such as tapping the right foot, tapping the left foot, slapping the shoulder, hands on hips, or any motions the leader can think of. The one who is IT guesses who is the leader. If IT guesses correctly, the leader becomes IT.

Leader and Class

The game may be played on a playground or in a gymnasium or classroom. The players who form the class stand in a row, facing the one who stands in the front, as the leader. The leader throws a beanbag, if little children are playing, or a ball to each in succession. If any child fails to catch the beanbag he must go to the foot of the class, that is, the end of the line. If the leader fails to catch the beanbag as it is thrown back, he must go to the foot also, and then the one who was at the head of the class or line takes his place. The game continues thus indefinitely.

Additional Comments:
- The underhand throw is recommended as being most practical. The activity leader should be careful that some children do not purposely throw poorly in order to make the game leader miss. The unfairness of this method of gaining the desired position should be emphasized.

Who Has the Bell (Jingle Bells)

One child, IT, is sent from the room. While he is out a tiny bell is given to another child. All of the children sit with their hands under desks. As IT comes back into the room the child who has the bell lets it jingle just a little. Whenever he has a chance, he jingles the bell until the one who is IT discovers who has the bell. The one who had the bell becomes IT and the bell is given to a new child.

Fox and Farmer

The players stand in a circle with arms stretched out sideways, resting on each other's shoulders, thus making a wide distance between the players. One player is chosen for the runner (fox) and one for the chaser (farmer). The game starts with the fox weaving in and out between the players or dashing across the circle in any way he sees fit. The farmer must always follow the same route. If the fox is caught, he joins the circle. The chaser then becomes the runner and chooses another for the chaser.

The leader may call time and choose two different players as runner and chaser if the game becomes too long. There also can be two or more sets of runners and chasers in very large groups.

Automobiles

Players number off, one to four or six, according to the size of the group and get into a circle formation. Number ones are Fords, twos Chevrolets, and so on. IT stands in the middle of the circle and calls the name of an automobile, such as Ford, and all Fords run counterclockwise around the circle and return to their original place and dash to the center to touch IT. The first runner to touch IT wins the Ford race. When each type of automobile has been called and the race run, the starter calls, "All winners," and this race determines the big winner.

Variations:
- This game may be played using the names of candy bars, cartoon characters, or airplanes.

Squirrels in the Trees

This game is played with 10 or more players, divided into groups of three. Two players within each group join raised hands to form a tree. The third player, the squirrel, stands within the tree. (Any extra players are also squirrels, but without trees.) At a given signal (clapped hands or blown whistle) all the squirrels must leave their trees and run for another one. The squirrels who are without trees after the change go to the center of the playing area. They stay there until the signal to change is repeated. Then they try again to find an unoccupied tree. The players should change roles after awhile, so trees can play the role of the squirrels and the squirrels become the trees.

Fox Trail (Fox and Geese)

A large circle from 15 to 30 feet in diameter should be marked on the ground or gym floor and crossed with intersecting lines like the spokes of a wheel, there being about five such lines (10 spokes). The more players there are, the larger the circle and the greater the number of spokes; but there is no fixed relation between the number of spokes and players. If played in the snow, this diagram may be trampled down with the feet; if on the fresh earth or sand, it may be drawn with a stick; or if in the gym, marked with chalk.

One player is chosen to be IT or the hunter. He stands in the center of the circle. The other players scatter around the rim and are the foxes. The object of the game is for the foxes to cross the wheel to some opposite point without being tagged by the hunter. (The player who is IT may be the hunter and chase foxes or he may be the fox and chase the geese.) The players may run only the prescribed trails, that is, on the lines of the diagram. They may run only straight across. The hunter changes places with anyone whom he tags.

Good Morning

One player chooses to be IT, and stands with his eyes closed and with his back turned toward the rest of the group. Someone selected by the leader says, "Good morning, Jim" (or whatever the child's name may be). To which IT replies, "Good morning, Suzy," giving the name of the person who he thinks addressed him. He may have three guesses and if he guesses correctly, he continues to be IT. If he fails on the third guess the one who spoke to him becomes IT.

Additional Comments:
- The leader should indicate to the child selected to say, "Good morning," by beckoning to the child or by nodding his head. The selection should be made quietly.
- The leader should appeal to fair play to maintain absolute quiet during the game. The children will be quiet as they learn it is more fun if everyone keeps very still.

Bird, Beast, Fish

The players form a three-deep circle. The players in the inner circle are birds, middle are beasts, and the outside are fish. IT is in the middle and he will call a name—bird, beast, or fish. The group which he names must all change places. When the group is changing, IT runs to an empty place and the person left without a place becomes IT.

Spider and Flies

The leader will draw two parallel lines about 60 feet apart. These are the goal lines. Players (flies) stand in a single circle in the area between the goal lines. The spider squats in the center of the circle. Skipping clockwise in the circle, the flies move around the spider. The flies say, "Buzz! Buzz! Buzz!" as they skip. Suddenly the spider says, "Into my web," and jumps up. Immediately he starts chasing the flies who scurry to either one of the goal lines. Anyone the spider tags goes into the web (center of the circle), and becomes a spider. The uncaught flies return to form the circle around the spiders. The spiders squat until the head spider jumps up and says, "Into my web." All other spiders follow his actions and assist in catching the flies; they do not instigate the action. The last fly to lose his freedom becomes the spider for the next game.

Aisle Ball

All of the children will stand in multiple file formation. The leader will give one of the children a beanbag (or a soft ball such as tennis ball or a playground ball). At the signal to start, the player with the bag calls the name of some player in one of the adjoining files and tosses the bag to that player. This player catches it, calls the name of one of the players in an adjoining file and tosses it to that player. In this manner, the bag is tossed about. Each pass should be made with an underhand throw and only to players in the immediately adjacent file—either left or right. Any player dropping the bag or making a very poor pass secures the bag and tosses it to another player then goes to the back of his row. The players in this row move forward one place to fill the gap created by the player who went to the rear. The desirable places are, of course, at the head of each row. This game may be varied by having every other row face to the rear, or also by allowing the players to toss the bag two or three rows away. Two or three beanbags may be used in this game.

Squirrel and Nut

All of the players but one sit at their desks with heads bowed on their arms as though sleeping, but each with a hand outstretched. The other player, who is the squirrel, carries a "nut," runs on tiptoe up and down through the aisles, and at her discretion drops the nut into one of the waiting hands. The player who gets the nut at once jumps up from his seat and chases the squirrel, who is safe only when she reaches her nest (seat). Should the squirrel be caught before she reaches her nest, she must be the squirrel the second time. Otherwise the player who received the nut becomes the next squirrel.

It is scarcely necessary to say that the other players wake up to watch the chase.

Crossing the River

Two sheets of newspaper folded to a size a little larger than a player's foot are needed for each team.

This is a relay. The players get into file formation. The folded papers are chunks of "ice." On the signal to start, player Number One of each team puts one piece of paper on the floor and steps on it, puts another piece ahead and then steps on it. Then she retrieves the first piece, pushes it forward and steps on it. This continues until the player has reached the goal and returned. She then hands the papers to player Number Two. Anytime a player steps on the floor instead of the paper, she falls into the water, and must return to the starting line and try again. The first team finished wins.

The Guessing Blind Man

This game will acquaint the children with the rest of the members of their group and is a good learning experience. Players form a circle. The player who is IT is blindfolded. Then he is turned around three times. Meanwhile the rest of the players change places in the circle. IT asks, "What is your favorite color?" The person IT asks must answer and if IT can guess who answered, the player in the circle becomes the new blind man. Otherwise, the blindfolded person continues to be IT.

Bird Catcher

Two opposite corners are marked off at one end of a room, the one to serve as a "nest" for the birds and the other as a "cage." A mother bird is chosen and takes her place in the nest. Other players take the part of the bird catchers and stand midway between the nest and cage. If played in a schoolroom, the remaining players sit in their seats; if on a playground, they stand beyond a line at the farther end of the ground which is called "the forest." All of these players should be named for birds, several players taking the name of each bird. The naming of the players will be facilitated by doing it in groups. If in the classroom, each row may choose its name, after which the players would all change places so that all of the robins or orioles will not fly from the same locality.

The leader calls the name of a bird, whereupon all of the players who bear that name of a bird run from the forest to the nest, but the bird catchers try to intercept them. Should a bird be caught by a bird catcher, he is put in the cage, but a bird is safe from the bird catchers once he reaches the nest and the mother bird. The players should be taught to make the chase interesting by dodging in various directions, instead of running in a simple, straight line for the nest.

The distance of the bird catchers from the nest may be determined with a little experience, and adjustments may be necessary to place a handicap upon them to avoid the too easy capture of the birds.

Wolf and Pigs

The players are in free formation. One child is named the wolf and the rest are the pigs. The wolf and pigs have their goals at each end of the play area with the middle being the free area. The wolf stays behind his goal walking around freely. The pigs are out in the free area pretending to play. The leader waits and says, "The wolf is coming," at which signal the wolf chases the pigs and tries to tag them before they reach their goal. Any pigs caught are then wolves and help the wolf on his next raid. The game is repeated and ends before the children become tired.

Additional Comments:
- The leader should set the goals about 40 feet apart and encourage the pigs to tantalize the wolf. The leader may vary distance of his signal for a long or short chase. The children should spread out as much as possible.

Who Has Gone From the Room?

The players sit in their seats or in a circle. One child is IT. He closes his eyes while the leader indicates which child shall leave the room. After this child has left, the child who is IT opens his eyes and guesses who has gone. If he names the child correctly, that child is IT the next time. If he fails to name the child, he closes his eyes again, the child returns to the room, and IT opens his eyes and guesses who has returned. If he fails, he must be IT again.

Additional Comments:
- The leader may use this quiet game for a rest period between active games.
- A large group may be divided into smaller play groups with each group playing independently.

Back-to-Back

All the players except one are arranged in couples. The partners stand back-to-back with their elbows linked. The extra player does not have a partner. Upon a signal from the leader, all players change partners while the extra player attempts to get a partner. One player will be left without a partner each time. The game is repeated with the player without a partner giving the signal for the next change.

Additional Comments:
- The leader should spread the couples over the whole playing area, and stop the game occasionally to allow the couples to scatter over the area.
- The leader should urge the children to find a different partner each time the change is made.
- A whistle, clap, or the call, "Change," may be used as a signal.
- This game works well with large groups.
- The leader may use this game as an icebreaker game by calling, "Front-to-front." Each player turns around, shakes hands, and introduces himself to his partner. The leader then calls, "Back-to-back," (original position), and then, "Change."

Cat and Rat

The players stand in a circle formation. The leader selects one player to be the cat and one to be the rat. The cat is outside the circle and the rat is inside the circle. The following conversation takes place:

> THE CAT: "I am the cat."
> THE RAT: "I am the rat."
> THE CAT: "I will catch you."
> THE RAT: "No! You can't."

The cat then chases the rat, attempting to catch him. The circle protects the rat by letting him leave and enter the circle easily. The cat may also enter and leave the circle. When the cat tags the rat, the cat becomes the rat and he selects another child to be the cat.

Additional Comments:
- The leader should teach strategy such as dodging and making quick changes in direction. He or she should coach the players forming the circle to help or hinder the chase as they let the runner in or out of the circle.
- This is a circle game where all players need to be actively playing the game.

Fox and Squirrel

The formation for this game is the same as for Squirrels in the Trees. There is one extra squirrel and also a fox. The fox chases the extra squirrel, who is safe by going into a tree. The squirrel who was in the tree that the extra squirrel went into must leave his tree and be chased by the fox. The fox can tag only the squirrel outside of the tree. Any squirrel tagged fairly by the fox becomes the fox and the fox becomes the extra squirrel.

Additional Comments:
- The trees should be scattered widely over the play area.
- The players' should change places occasionally, so that all have an opportunity to be the squirrel.
- If the group is large, the leader may use several players to form each tree.
- The leader should warn the squirrels not to leave their trees until the extra squirrel enters their tree, and they then must leave at once.
- The leader should not let one child be the fox too long; rather, ask him to change places with another child if he is unable to tag anyone.

Gardener and the Rabbit

The players stand in a circle formation. One child, the rabbit, is inside the circle and another, the gardener, is outside the circle. This conversation takes place:

> GARDENER: "Who let you into my garden?"
> RABBIT: "No one."
> GARDENER: "I will chase you."
> RABBIT: "All right."

Then the rabbit leaves the inside of the circle as the gardener comes in and chases him out. The gardener must follow the rabbit leaving the circle through the same place and doing everything the rabbit does. The rabbit, doing stunts that the gardener must repeat, attempts to get back into the circle by entering through the same place through which he left, before the gardener tags him. If he is tagged, the rabbit becomes the gardener. If the rabbit is not tagged, the gardener remains the gardener and a new rabbit is chosen for the repetition of the game. If the gardener fails to perform any of the rabbit's stunts, he returns to the circle and the rabbit chooses a new gardener.

Additional Comments:
- The leader should prohibit unsafe stunts, but rather suggest stunts such as hopping, jumping, or going under or around objects.
- If the play area is extensive, the leader may limit the space within which the chase may take place.
- The leader should watch for signs of fatigue, and select a new gardener when a child has been unable to tag a rabbit.

Variations:
- The players may scatter over a limited play area and the game is played without a safety zone for the rabbit.

Have You Seen My Sheep?

The players sit or stand in circle formation. One player is IT; he goes around the outside of the circle, stops behind another player and says, "Have you seen my sheep?" The player in the circle replies, "What does he look like?" The child who is IT then describes another player in the circle, while the second player guesses who is being described. As soon as he guesses correctly, he chases the described person around the outside of the circle, trying to tag him before he can run around the circle and return to his place. If that player is tagged, he becomes IT, and if he is not tagged, the chaser is IT and the game is repeated. The original IT does not take part in this chase but steps into the circle in the place vacated by the chaser.

When the game is played in a classroom, the children sit in their seats. The goal is the vacated seat; and the child who is originally IT goes back to his own seat, being careful to stay out of the way of the chaser and the runner.

Additional Comments:
- The leader may suggest ways to describe a child such as color of clothes, hair, or eyes.
- The leader should demonstrate how to play the game before it is actually played.
- The leader should teach the children to listen carefully to the description and to be ready to run if they are described.

Hide-and-Seek

One player is IT and he stands at the goal (a tree or post) and the other players hide. While the others run and hide, he counts to 25. He then calls that he is coming and goes out to look for them. The first one who he finds is IT the next time the game is played. He continues the search until all are found.

Additional Comments:
- The leader should not use hiding games with large groups of children.
- A whistle or similar signal may be used to call players in who have not been found if the game drags.
- The leader should know his play area and forbid the use of undesirable hiding places. This should be explained carefully before playing a hiding game.
- Children like to play hide-and-seek games. They may need to be taught representative types of hiding games so that they know how to play these games in school and neighborhood groups.

Huckleberry Beanstalk

Some small object is hidden by the leader while the players are outside of the room. They are called in to hunt for the hidden object. Anyone seeing it takes his seat and calls, "Huckleberry beanstalk." The object of the game is not to be the last one to find the hidden object. Children will learn that they must not look at the hidden object as they say, "Huckleberry beanstalk."

Additional Comments:
- The leader should select an object which is different from anything else in the room. He should not hide it higher than the children's eye level.
- The leader may let the child who first spies the hidden object hide it the next time the game is played.
- When it is not convenient for the children to leave the room, the leader should instruct the players to close their eyes and put their heads on their desks as he hides the object.

Big Bear

One child is chosen to be the bear. He stands in his "den," about one third of the play space, marked off in the center of the play area. The bear is teased by the other players, who run across his den and call, "Big bear, big bear, can't catch anybody." The bear may tag anyone within his den, and he may take only three steps outside his den to tag the players. After taking three steps, he may hop on one foot. However, if he puts both feet down after he has taken three steps, the players may drive the bear back into his den to which he must return before he can tag anyone. He may return to his den to rest at any time. Anyone whom he tags becomes the bear. The game may be played with each player who is tagged assisting the bear in tagging the other players until they are all tagged.

Additional Comments:
- The leader should allow and encourage the bear to change from hopping on one foot to the other and remind the bear that he may return to his den to rest.
- If the group is large, the game may have several bears, each changing places with anyone whom he may tag.

Midnight

One player is the fox and the other players are the chickens. The fox is in his "den," a small area marked off at one end of the play space. The chickens approach his den asking, "What time is it?" The fox may answer any clock time. When he answers, "Midnight," that is his signal that he is going to chase the chickens. At the signal the chickens run for safety. They are safe when they reach a specified area or goal line at the opposite end of the play space. Any who are caught by the fox before they reach safety are taken to his den and they assist in catching the chickens when the fox again calls his signal. The chickens approach the fox's den and the game continues until all of the players are tagged.

Additional Comments:
- If the group is large, containing more than 10 players, the game becomes confusing when too many are tagged. So, with a large group, the first one tagged each time may become the fox.
- The leader should urge the children to dare to go close to the fox's den.

Partner Tag

Each player links one elbow with a partner. Two children are without partners: one is the chaser and he tries to tag the other who is the runner. The runner is safe when he links elbows with any player. The partner of the player with whom he links elbows immediately becomes the runner and is chased. When a chaser tags a runner, the runner becomes the chaser and the chaser becomes the runner.

Additional Comments:
- The leader should spread the players out over the playing area. It is easy for the runner to save himself from being tagged, so one child should not be the chaser too long. The leader should stop the game, let the two players link elbows, and select two other players as the new chaser and runner.

Variations:
- The game may be played with partners linking elbows as they stand side-by-side in a single circle. The chaser and runner run around the circle and in either direction.

Run for Your Supper

Players are in a circle formation, one player being IT. He goes around the outside of the circle and, stopping between any two players says, "Run for your supper." The two players turn away from the player who is IT and run in opposite directions around the circle, each attempting to get back first into the place in the circle vacated by the other. The last one back is IT for the repetition of the game.

Additional Comments:
- The leader should make it clear that the players do not return to their own places but to the place vacated by the other player. Otherwise, they will collide with each other in trying to get into their own place.
- Children may want to be IT, and they may deliberately avoid getting back first. In that case, the leader may change the objective of the game and allow the first one back to be IT for the repetition of the game.

Shadow Tag

This game is played like simple tag, *except* that the chaser tags the runner by stepping on his shadow. He calls the name of the child upon whose shadow he stepped and that child becomes IT. Shadow Tag may be played with the players safe when standing on any shadow.

Additional Comments:
- The leader may vary the kinds of shadows to be used as safeties, such as trees and building shadows.

Spin the Can

The children stand or sit in a circle and each child is given a number. One child is IT. She spins a can, bottle, or football on the floor in the center of the circle as she calls a number. The child whose number she called tries to catch the can before it stops spinning. If he is successful he may be IT and the game is repeated.

The game may be changed so that if the child does not catch the can then he is IT.

Additional Comments:
- The leader should not allow the children to play the game for a long period of time, as most of the players are inactive.
- The leader may increase the size of the circle to increase the skill needed in catching the can.

Tommy Tiddler

A circle 10 feet in diameter is marked on the playing area. All but one of the players stands outside of the circle. The extra player is Tommy Tiddler and he stays inside of the circle. Tommy is supposed to guard huge stores of treasures. At a signal, the players enter the circle (Tommy Tiddler's Land) and attempt to steal the treasure. As they enter, they shout, "Here I stand on Tommy Tiddler's Land stealing gold and silver." Tommy attempts to tag one of these players. Any player tagged by Tommy while standing on Tommy's land exchanges places with him and immediately the game continues.

Additional Comments:
- The leader should urge the players to venture as near to Tommy Tiddler as they can without being tagged.

Touch Ball

Players are in a circle formation. One child, who is IT, stands inside of the circle. A ball is passed from player to player around the circle and across the circle. The child who is IT must try to touch the ball. When he does, the child who threw the ball or touched it last becomes IT.

Additional Comments:
- A large group may be divided into several small circles of players, each with a ball.
- The leader may teach the children to throw accurately and encourage them to increase distance in throwing across the circle.

Water Sprite

Goal lines are marked across both ends of the play area. One child is chosen as the sprite and he stands in the center of the play area. The other players are divided into two groups, each behind its goal line at one end of the play area. The sprite calls the name of one of the players, who immediately calls the name of one of the players on the opposite goal line. These two players change goals while the sprite tries to tag one of them before they reach the opposite goal line. If he tags one, he changes places with him and goes to the goal line toward which the tagged player was running, while the child who was tagged becomes IT.

Additional Comments:
- The water sprite should stand in the center until both names are called. The leader should teach the players to run immediately after both names are called.
- The leader should suggest that the players call the names of children who have not been called previously.
- The game may be played with numbers instead of names to introduce a different element into the game. This is also helpful when playing the game with children who do not know the names of their playmates.

Who Is Knocking at My Door?

The players sit in their own seats while the child who is IT sits in a chair in the front of the room, with his back to the players. Another player is chosen by the leader to go and knock on the floor behind the chair of the child who is IT. Upon hearing the knock IT asks, "Who is knocking at my door?" The knocker answers, "It is I." The child who is IT is allowed three trials to guess who is knocking. If he guesses correctly, the knocker becomes IT. If he cannot guess, he may look and he is then IT again.

Additional Comments:
- The leader may limit the number of trials to one or two guesses when the group is small, and allow the knocker to disguise his voice.

Shoe Laugh

Players are sitting in a circle. The leader throws a shoe into the center. If it falls right side up, all the players have to laugh, and if it falls upside down, all have to point toward it very seriously. If anyone does not do the right thing, he has to give a forfeit, and after the game, must redeem it. *Forfeit* is a term used to refer to *any* consequence the leader or the group decide, resulting from "an error" of some type. It could be doing a push-up, singing a song, twirling three times, and taking shoes off and putting them back on. *Forfeit* is a term which is more neutral than the term *penalty*. Therefore if a leader wants to use a forfeit, he or she can choose what it will be. Forfeits can be used as a deterrent *not* to make an error, or they can act as motivators. Forfeits, if used properly, can also bring positive attention to the individual. The leader, knowing members of his or her group will decide which forfeit is or is not appropriate.

Flying Dutchman

All the players except two join hands in a circle. The two who remain outside join hands, walk around the outside of the circle, and tag the joined hands of any two players. These players immediately chase the taggers around the circle, trying to catch them before they get into the space originally occupied by the chasers. Tagged players must keep their hands clasped while running. There are no partners because a player may have to run with either of his neighbors.

Air Balloon

The group is divided into equally numbered circles and each group has a balloon. On the count of three, each group plays against the others to see who can keep the balloon in the air the longest. Each player may tap the balloon only once, but may tap it again after another player has.

Variations:
• Music may be played and each player taps to the rhythm.

Bull in the Ring

If there are not too many, the players form one circle or ring. If there are more than 15, they should form two circles. One player is chosen to be the bull, and those in the circle clasp hands as firmly as possible in an effort to keep the bull from breaking through and escaping. If he should manage to do so, all in the circle give chase, and the one who catches him may be the bull the next time.

Butterflies

One child is the butterfly catcher and stands in front of others. Another child is selected to be the first butterfly, and she runs around the room waving her arms slowly up and down. During her run, she taps others on the head, and they fly around the room in a line behind the first. When there are six or seven butterflies, the leader taps on the wall and the butterfly catcher gives chase. The butterflies must fly home before they are caught. The first person caught is the butterfly catcher for the next game.

Sore Spot Tag

This game is played as ordinary tag except that IT must hold one hand on the spot (part of his body) where he was tagged. Any player running outside the playing area automatically becomes IT.

Additional Comments:
- If the game moves too slowly, the leader may make more than one player IT.

Take Me Home

One child is chosen to be a policeman. She is sent from the room while all the other players become "lost" (sit in seats that are not their own). When the policeman is called back into the room, all the children say, "We are lost and we want to go home." The policeman takes the hand of one child at a time and tries to put him in his proper seat. If she puts the child in the wrong seat, the child begins to "cry" and runs away from the policeman. Then the policeman catches him and tries to put him in the proper seat again. This continues until every child in the room has been returned "home."

Jacob and Rachel

This game requires two clean handkerchiefs or other blindfolds. All players but two join hands in a circle. The odd players, Jacob and Rachel, are blindfolded and in the center of the circle. The object of the game is for Jacob to catch Rachel, first locating her by the sound of her voice. Jacob calls out: "Rachel, where art thou?" "Here I am, Jacob," Rachel replies. She may evade him in any way but must stay in the circle. When Rachel is caught, a new Rachel and Jacob are chosen.

Jack Be Nimble

An upright object representing a candlestick is placed in front of the room. The players form a file within 15 feet of the object. At a signal, the players move forward one at a time, leap over the object, and re-form in a file at the opposite side of the room. As each player runs forward to jump over the object, each repeats the jingle, "Jack be nimble, Jack be quick, Jack jump over the candlestick" (or whatever he or she jumps over which represents the candlestick). When a child knocks over the candlestick, the players halt for a moment until the one who knocked it over sets it up.

Freeze Tag

The players stand freely around the room or play area. One player is IT and she chases the other players and tries to tag them. Once a player is tagged, he must stand frozen in place. However, if a player who hasn't been tagged by IT can come and touch him, he is unfrozen and can resume playing. IT tries to catch as many players as possible. When she catches them all, the last one caught is IT for the next game.

Blind Bell

All the players but one are blindfolded and scattered about a designated area. The one who is not blindfolded carries a bell loosely in one hand, so that it will ring with every step. If desired, this bell may be hung around the neck on a string or ribbon. The blindfolded players try to catch the one with the bell who will have to use considerable alertness to keep out of the way. Whoever catches the bellman changes places with him.

Call Number (Duck, Duck, Goose)

The players are in a circle formation. One person is IT and the rest of the players sit down. Each is given a number from one to as many as there are players. The person who is IT walks around the circle. The leader then calls a number, and that person has to get up and run around the circle. She must sit down in her place before the person who is IT tags her. If the runner is tagged, she becomes IT and the game continues.

Additional Comments:
- The leader should demonstrate the game first.
- The leader should teach the children to listen carefully to their numbers.
- Duck, Duck, Goose is played in the same manner except IT taps the head of each player saying either, "Duck" or "Goose." When IT taps the head of a player and says, "Goose," that player gets up and chases IT.

Blackboard Relay

Blackboard relay is played in a relay formation similar to a simple relay. However, instead of crossing a goal, each player writes a number on the blackboard just in front of his team. The last child must add all of the numbers written on the board by his team. The team wins which finishes first with its numbers correctly added and with no fouls against it.

Additional Comments:
- The leader may refer to additional comments with the description of Automobile Relay.

Variations:
- The players may write, instead of numbers, the names of objects in the room, colors, or trees. There must be no duplication in the list of any team.

Blindman's Bluff

The players are in a circle formation with one player, the blind man, in the center and blindfolded. The circle moves around until the blind man claps his hands. He then points toward the circle of players and calls the name of any animal. The player to whom he is pointing must make the noise like that animal. The blind man must guess who the player is. Three trials are given to him. If he is successful in guessing the name of the player, that player becomes the blind man. If he does not guess correctly, he is the blind man again and the game is repeated.

Additional Comments:
- A clean paper sack pulled over the child's head may be used for a blindfold.
- This game lacks activity, but it is fun. It can be used as a rest game between more active games.

Variations:
- The animal noises are omitted and the child to whom the blind man points steps into the circle. The blind man must catch him and then, still blindfolded, guess who he is.

Automobile Relay

Automobile relay is played as a simple relay race. However, each team chooses the name of an automobile as the name of its team. Automobile Relay may be varied for classroom use as follows: alternate rows; play at the same time and, in turn, beginning with the first child in each row, each child leaves his seat from the left-hand side, runs forward and around his own row of seats and returns to his own seat on the left-hand side, tagging the next runner. This continues until the last child has run. The row which finishes first with the last runner in his seat is the winning team.

Additional Comments:
- The leader may allow each row of seats to choose its own name.

Variations:
- The leader may dramatize the auto race by changing circumstances. The relay may be run with horns sounding on each turn (it will be noisy), or with flat tires and the runners hopping in after the last turn.

Corner Tag

Each player has a "corner" or a definite goal such as a tree or corner of a building. One player is without a corner and he is IT. He has a large, soft ball and he attempts to get a goal by "tagging" another player. He tags a player by hitting him below the waist with his ball when the player is not on a corner. Players change corners at will but all players must change when the player who is IT calls, "Corner." When a player is tagged fairly, he becomes IT and the game continues.

Additional Comments:
- A volleyball or red playground ball should be used.
- The leader should insist that the ball must hit players below the waist.
- This game should be played with very small groups of children. This is a good game to teach children to use for home or neighborhood play.

Boiler Burst

The children are grouped around one player who is telling a story. Suddenly in his story he calls, "Boiler burst!" This is a signal that he is going to chase them. The players scatter and run for a goal line or area designated as a safety zone. The first one caught starts the game again with others grouped around him. The story is continued and the game repeated.

Additional Comments:
- The children may continue the same story or the caught child may start another story.

Variations:
- The players are seated. They must change seats on the signal and the child calling the signal tries to get a seat as they change. The child left without a seat continues the story.

Boundary Ball

The play space, about the size of a basketball court, is divided into three equal areas: one central and two end areas. The players are divided into two teams with one team in each end area. The object of the game is to throw, roll, or bounce a ball over the opponent's rear boundary line.

A player from each team stands on his own rear boundary line with a ball. On the signal to start, the two balls are thrown into play by these two players. Thereafter, the balls are thrown from the place where they are intercepted within the end area. No ball can be played from outside the boundary lines of the end areas. A ball which goes out of bounds is recovered by a nearby player and brought just inside the end area at the point where it went out. The central area is neutral and is considered out of bounds. The team that first gets a ball over the opponent's rear boundary line wins the game.

After the players become skillful, the game may be scored. One point is scored for each ball thrown over the opponent's rear boundary line, and the team first scoring five points wins the game. After each score, the ball is recovered, brought back just inside the boundary line, and put into play again.

Additional Comments:
- This game should be played with a volleyball or a large playground ball. The leader should start the game with only one ball, and then use two balls when he is sure that the children are alert in catching and dodging balls.

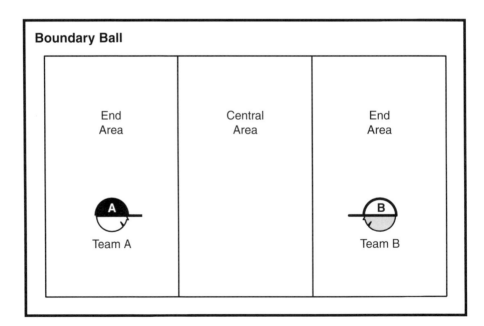

Boundary Ball

| End Area | Central Area | End Area |

A — Team A

B — Team B

- The leader should teach the children how to throw a ball hard and fast, and how speed gives distance to a throw.
- If children have trouble in getting a ball across the goal, the leader may shorten the distance between the two rear boundary lines.
- The leader should adjust the size of the play area, the types of throws, and scoring to the ability of the groups playing.

Catch the Cane

The players stand in a circle formation with the player who is IT in the center. All players including IT, are given a number. The child who is IT holds a cane, with the tip of a finger, in a upright position with one end on the floor. He calls a number as he lets go of the cane. The player whose number is called attempts to catch the cane before it drops to the floor. If he fails to catch it, he is IT and the game is repeated. If he catches the cane, he returns to his place in the circle and the first child is IT again.

Additional Comments:
- This game may be played with an ordinary smooth stick, a wand, or a three-foot long broom handle for the cane.
- The game may be changed by saying that the child may be IT if he catches the cane before it falls.
- If the players catch the cane too easily, the leader may increase the size of the circle. If they are not catching it, the circle may be made smaller.
- The leader may teach the children to keep their eye on the ball (in this case their eye on the cane) and be ready with their weight on their toes and with one foot ahead of the other.

Center Base

The players stand in a circle formation. One player is IT and he stands in the center of the circle. He tosses a ball to a player in the circle who catches it, brings it to the center, and places it in the base. The base is a small circle marked in the center of the circle of players. After he has placed the ball in the base, he chases the player who threw the ball to him. Both the runner and the chaser must leave the circle through the space left in the circle by the player catching the ball, and the runner is safe by coming back into the circle through this same space and touching the ball. If the chaser tags the runner, the runner is IT another time. If he does not tag the runner, the chaser is IT and the game is repeated.

Additional Comments:
- The leader may teach the runners to lure the chaser away from the open space in the circle.
- The leader may select a new player to start the game with each repetition in order to bring more children into the activity of the game. He may encourage the child who is IT to throw to a different player (one who has not played) with each repetition of the game.

Hill Dill

The child who is IT stands in the center of the play area while the other players stand behind one of the goal lines marked across the ends of the play area. The group is divided so that about half of the players are behind each goal line. The child who is IT calls "Hill dill, come over the hill!" On this signal, the players run across the center space to the opposite goals while the child who is IT tries to tag them. The players who are tagged go to the center and help tag the remaining players. The game is continued, with the original IT giving the signal each time, until all of the players are tagged.

Additional Comments:
- The distance between the goals should be approximately 40 feet.

Variations:
- The first child tagged in each chase becomes IT, taking the place of the child who was in the center.
- The game starts with several players as IT in the center. Then, when a player is tagged, he takes the place of the child in the center who tagged him. One of the children in the center must be selected to call the signals or the leader may call the signal each time.

Eraser Relay

The children remain in their seats and the teams are designated by the rows across the room. A clean blackboard eraser is placed on the floor in the outside aisle beside the seat of each child in the right-hand row of seats. At a signal, each child in this row picks up the eraser in his right hand, places it in his left hand, and places it on the floor to his left, where it is picked up in the right hand of the next child and thus passed across the width of the room. The team wins which finishes first with the blackboard eraser on the floor in the left-hand outside aisle.

Additional Comments:
- Beanbags may be used instead of blackboard erasers. Dusty erasers should not be used. The leader should not allow the blackboard eraser or beanbag to be thrown.

Nose and Toes Tag

This game is played as a simple tag game, except that the runner may escape being tagged by grasping his nose with one hand and his foot with the other hand. A player who is tagged becomes IT and the game is continued.

Additional Comments:
- The players should be scattered over the playing area. The leader should explain that the safety position may be assumed in a squatting position or while standing on one foot. It is safe to take the squat or knee-bend position after running fast. The leader should not permit bumping or pushing of the players who are in the safety position. He should not let a chaser wait for a player to lose his balance or tire from holding his position; rather encourage fair play and the fun of chasing.

Pinch-Oh!

The players stand in a line with their backs toward the goal and with hands joined behind their backs. One child, selected to be IT stands facing the line of players, and about 10 feet from them, waiting to chase them to the goal. The first child in the line pinches or squeezes the hand of his neighbor as he calls, "Pinch!" The pinch is passed on from player to player until it reaches the child at the opposite end of the line. The last child, after receiving the pinch, calls, "Oh!" This is the signal for the players to drop hands and run to the goal line across the opposite end of the play area. The child who is IT tries to tag the players before they reach the goal line. The first child whom he tags becomes IT and the game is repeated.

Additional Comments:
- The leader should teach the players to turn in the same direction and to turn and run at the same time. If they turn to the left, the first step toward the goal will be on the left foot and the push off will be done with the right foot. If each player puts his right hand behind his back, more room will be allowed and fewer collisions will result as all players turn to the left to take off. The leader should let the children practice this turn before playing the game.

Posture Relay

The players are arranged in file formation, as for a simple relay race. The first player in each file has a beanbag. At the signal to start, he puts it on his head, runs to the goal line and back, and hands the beanbag to the next player. Each team member in turn, receives the beanbag, places it on his head, and runs, until the whole team has participated. The team finishing first wins the relay.

The hands may be used only to place the beanbag on the head and to pass it on to the next player. The runner cannot leave the starting line before the beanbag is placed on his head and he cannot hold the beanbag as he is running.

Additional Comments:
- The leader should let the children practice walking with the beanbag on the head before putting the stunt into a relay. A book may be used in place of the beanbag.
- This game should not be played when there is a possibility of any children in the group having head lice.

Posture Tag

The players are scattered over the play area. Two players are chosen to start: one is IT and the other is the runner, and each places a beanbag on his head. The runner may transfer his beanbag to any other player's head and that player is then the runner. When a runner is tagged, he becomes IT and the chaser becomes the runner. The hands may be used only to place the beanbag on the head; the child cannot hold the beanbag as he is running.

Additional Comments:
- This game should not be played when there is a possibility of any children in the group having head lice.

Pum-Pum-Pullaway

The players are behind a goal line marked across one end of the play area. Another goal line is marked at the opposite end. One player, who is IT, stands in the center of the play area and calls, "Pum-pum-pullaway. Come, or I will pull you away." At this signal, all the other players must run to the opposite goal while IT tries to tag them before they reach the goal. Those who are tagged stay in the center and help to tag the remaining players as the game is continued. The object is to be the last one caught.

Red Light, Green Light

The player selected to be IT stands on a goal line marked across one end of the play area. The other players are on a starting line at the opposite end. The child who is IT calls, "Green light." He turns his back to the players and counts aloud, "1–2–3–4–5–6–7–8–9–10–red light." The players start on the signal, *green light,* and run toward the goal line, but they must stop on the words *red light.* On this signal, IT turns to face the players. If he sees a player moving his feet, he sends her back to the starting line. Each player tries to be the first to reach the goal line. However, the game continues until all are over the goal line. The first player over the line is IT as the game is repeated.

Additional Comments:
- The leader should teach the players to watch all of the group when they are IT and to accept the decision of the child who is IT when they are told to return because they were moving.

Variations:
- The players start at the goal line, proceed to the designated line, and then return to the goal line.

Simple Dodge Ball

This is an informal type of dodge ball. The players are arranged with about two thirds of the players in a large circle and the remaining one third inside the circle. Those standing in the circle formation have a playground ball with which they attempt to hit those inside the circle. A hit must be below the waist. When he is hit, a player joins the circle formation. The last one remaining in the center wins the game. The game should be repeated until all players have had an opportunity to be inside the circle at the beginning of the game. Whenever a ball goes outside of the circle, a nearby player recovers it and brings it to the circle or passes it to a player in the circle.

Additional Comments:
- The leader should caution the players continuously to hit below the waist, and to keep their eyes on the ball whether they are in the circle formation or inside the circle.

Variations:
- The leader may place fewer players inside the circle—about three out of a group of 12 or 15 players. Whenever a player is hit fairly, he exchanges places with the player in the circle who hit him. The changes should be made quickly to keep the game moving.

Simple Relay

Players are arranged in file formation behind a starting line. Each file represents a team and all files are composed of an equal number of players. A goal is designated approximately 30 feet from the starting line. The goal may be a line or an object such as a stool, chair, or Indian club in front of each file. The first player in each file remains with one foot in contact with the starting line until the signal to start the relay is given by the leader. As the signal is given, the first player in each file line, runs to the goal (crosses the goal line or runs around the object), returns to the starting line, tags the second player, and goes to the right of his team to take his place at the end of the file. Each player, in turn, is tagged, runs, tags the next player, and takes his place at the end of the file as he completes his run. The winning team finishes first with all the players back in their original places in the file provided that no fouls have been made by the team.

It is a foul for a player to start before he is tagged, or to fail in observing the goal rule. The files move forward each time a new runner starts; the next runner contacts the starting line ready to run when he is tagged by the previous runner. Players may not be required to get into formation at the end of the relay and the team wins when its last runner crosses the starting line first on the return from the goal line. However, it facilitates judging the finish when players are required to be in file formation at the end of the game. It is even simpler to judge if the players are asked to sit down in their places as the team finishes.

Additional Comments:

- The leader should keep teams small, using from three to five teams with five or six players on each team. Extra players may judge fouls and the finish. The leader may insist that all teams finish the relay even when it seems that another team has won.
- The leader should avoid "touching the wall" as a goal, as this practice is a safety hazard for children who have not learned to stop and turn after running fast.
- The leader should use guards for the first relay the children play. A guard is appointed for each file. He stands in front of the starting line at the right-hand side of the first player, and holds his right hand in front of the runner who is waiting to run. The runner cannot pass the guard's hand until he has been tagged. The leader should change guards after each game so that they may have an opportunity to run. The guards may be eliminated after the group has learned to play.

Still Pond

One player is IT and is blindfolded. The other players group around him and ask, "How many horses in your father's stable?" IT answers, "Three." The group asks, "What colors are they?" IT says, "Black, white, and gray." The players turn the player who is IT around three times, saying, "Turn around three times and catch whom you may." They scatter away from IT, but must stop when he calls, "Still pond, no more moving." Each player now is allowed only three steps. The player who is blindfolded attempts to touch one of the players. When he touches one, he must guess whom he has touched. If he guesses correctly, that player is IT for the next time. If he misses in his guess, he must touch another player and guess again.

If a player is touched, he cannot try to get away, but must allow the player who is IT to try to guess who he is by feeling his clothing, height, and hair.

Additional Comments:
- The leader should teach the players to dodge and move without taking their limited number of steps to avoid being tagged.
- A clean paper sack pulled down over the head may be used for the blindfold.
- The leader should see that no obstructions are in the way of the blindfolded child and continuously watch the player to be sure that he is safe.
- The leader should teach the children to play games wherein a player is blindfolded only in safe areas.
- There should not be any steps or inclines, any dangerous obstruction, or any traffic.

Stone

A goal is marked at both ends of the play area. One player is the stone. He squats down in the center of the play area with the other players around him. They skip and run around him while he sits very still. Then he calls, "Stone." He jumps up to chase them and they run to the goal at either end of the room or play area. Anyone tagged before reaching a goal becomes a stone and squats down in the center with the original stone. The other players move around the center again. No stone can chase until the original stone calls, "Stone." Then all attempt to tag players before they reach one of the goals. The game is continued until all are caught.

Additional Comments:
- When the game is started, the players may join hands in a circle. As the circle gets smaller, they will not be able to join hands and move around the center players, but they must keep within the center of the play area.

- The leader should teach the players how to get a quick takeoff from a crouch-start position. The players may plan cues to indicate when the stone is going to call his signal. The cue may be something he says or the direction he faces.

Note:
- The number of players governs the size of the groups. The game is for a fairly small number of players, for example, three groups of four or five players.

Indian Running

Five or six players are chosen to leave the room. These players arrange themselves in any order, return to the room running once around it, then leave again. Then they return and other players must name the correct order of the players as they ran around the room. The child who is successful may choose four or five other children to leave with him and the game is played again.

Additional Comments:
- The children should wait until called upon to name the order of the runners. The five or six runners should go to the front of the room where the other children, in their turns, try to place them in the correct order.

I Say Stoop

The players stand in the aisles facing the front of the room. The leader stands in front of the players and gives the command, "I say stoop!" or "I say stand!" The players follow the leader's commands and not his actions. He may stoop when he says stand or stand when he says stoop. Anyone not following the command becomes IT and takes the place of the leader. The stoop can be a deep knee-bend position.

Additional Comments:
- If the children tend to miss intentionally in order to become IT, the leader may change the rules of the game. Perhaps the child who misses may be required to drop out of the game. This is not usually a good procedure, as it takes the child out of the activity.

Variations:
- The leader may use commands such as "I say up! I say down! Jack says up! Jack says down!"

- The leader may make a rule that the players follow the commands only when *I say* precedes the command, and they must not act when the command is just *stoop* or *stand.*

Keep It up

The players form two or more teams with five or six players on a team and get into small circles. Each team has a volleyball, playground ball, balloon, or earthball. Upon a signal, the ball is tossed into play by a team member. The players attempt to keep their team's ball in the air by batting it with open hands and the team that keeps its ball up the longest wins a point. The team that earns the most points within the playing period wins the game.

Additional Comments:
- The game may be played informally and without team competition until the players become acquainted with the skill of hitting the ball into the air with the open hand.
- The players may not catch and toss the ball during play. It must be hit as a setup is played in volleyball.
- The leader may change the method of scoring by declaring the team that first earns five points the winner.

Spud

The players are in the center of the play area and grouped around a single player, IT, who has a ball. He throws the ball above his head to a designated height. As the ball is in the air the players scatter away from IT. IT catches the ball and calls, "Spud." Everyone must stop wherever he is as soon as IT calls. The player who is IT throws the ball, attempting to hit one of the players below the waist. If he hits a player fairly, the player who was hit is IT and the game starts again from the center. If he fails to hit a player, IT runs and recovers the ball while the players scatter again. Upon recovering the ball, IT calls, "Spud." Again everyone must stop wherever he is. IT again attempts to hit a player by throwing the ball. If he hits a player, the player is IT. If he fails to hit a player, he recovers the ball as the players scatter again. If IT fails on this, the third trial, he brings the ball back to the center. A new IT is selected and the game begins again from the center. Note that whenever a player is hit and becomes IT or when a new IT is selected, the game begins again from the center of the play area. The players may scatter as soon as IT moves to recover the ball after the first and second trials.

A player who misses after three trials is marked as a spud. Later he is made "to run the gauntlet" or pay a forfeit.

Additional Comments:
- This game should be played with a large soft ball such as a volleyball or playground ball.
- The leader should teach the players how to toss a ball high into the air, and designate the height of the toss.
- The leader should insist that players hit below the waist.

Variations:
- The players return to the center after each trial, and IT is allowed only two trials.
- IT throws the ball against a wall and catches it instead of tossing the ball above the head.
- Each participant is given a number. When IT tosses the ball into the air, he calls a number, not his own. The owner of the number becomes the new IT and must retrieve the ball. When the new IT controls the ball, he yells, "Spud."

Touch off

Two teams are lined up on opposite goal lines, one at each end of the play area. The first child from Team One advances as a scout to the second team. Each player in that team holds out his right hand. The scout touches the hands of these players. Deciding upon a player whom he wants to chase him, he gives that player a slap on the hand. The chase begins as the player whose hand was slapped attempts to tag the player from Team One before he can return to Team One's goal line. If he is tagged, he must join the other team. Play continues with the first child from Team Two as a scout. Play repeats by alternating sides until each child has had a turn as scout. The winning team has more players at the end of the game.

Additional Comments:
- The scout may attempt to trick the players by pretending that he is going to slap a player's hand and then barely touch it.

Variations:
- A point may be awarded to the team for tagging the runner returning to his goal. A captain is appointed for each team and he selects the scout to send from his team each time. The players return to their own team after each run. The team wins that has earned more points within the playing period, or that first wins five points.

Two Deep

The players form a circle facing the center of the circle. One player is selected as the chaser and another as the runner. The chaser attempts to tag the runner as he runs around the circle in either direction. The runner saves himself from being tagged by stepping in front of one of the players in the circle; that player immediately becomes the runner and the chaser tries to tag him. When a chaser tags the runner, the runner becomes the chaser and the game continues.

Additional Comments:
- Players should not cut across the circle except to step in front of a player.

Wood Tag

In Wood Tag the players are chased by one player designated as IT. Any player touching wood is safe from being tagged.

Hand Tag

A player is safe when hanging by his hand or hands with feet off the ground. This is a successful game when there are trees and playground apparatus from which the players may hang safely.

Base Tag

The player is safe while touching marked bases.

Additional Comments:
- There are many safety tag games and safeties may be varied according to the type and location. The leader may choose to try Tree Tag, Iron Tag, o Line Tag, wherein the players are safe in touching a tree, iron, or a line.

Trades

The players are divided into two groups. A goal line is marked across each end of the play area and one group stands behind each goal line. The first group decides upon a "trade." The players leave their goal and go to the opposite end of the play area, calling, "Here we come." The second group asks, "Where from?"

> FIRST GROUP: "New Orleans."
> SECOND GROUP: "What is your trade?"
> FIRST GROUP: "Lemonade."
> SECOND GROUP: "Show us some."

Then the first group pantomimes its trade while the second tries to guess the trade. If they guess correctly, they immediately give chase while the first group runs for its goal. Any players who are tagged before reaching their goal become members of the tagging team. The game is repeated with the second group choosing a trade. The players must maintain contact with their goal line until the chase begins.

Additional Comments:
- If the players need help in selecting trades, the leader may suggest some such as washing dishes, making a cake, sweeping the floor, laying bricks, fishing, and sawing wood.

Around the Bases

Any number of players, divided into two, three, or four equal teams, may play this game. The group is divided into even teams, using home, first, second, and third base as team stations. At a given signal, the first member of each team leaves his station and runs the bases. When he returns to his original station, he touches the number two player, and the game continues.

If there are a limited number of players, one or two teams may be eliminated with teams placed at home and second base only.

Plug

Five players make a plug (horse) by locking their arms around the waist of the player in front. The other players form a circle around plug. They are the throwers and throw a Nerf ball or playground ball at plug's tail. When hit below the waist, plug's tail becomes a thrower. The player that "tagged" the tail becomes the head of the horse and the game repeats.

Additional Comments:
- The leader should encourage the players to pass the ball around the circle to find an opportunity to hit plug's tail.

Jack Frost

A 20-foot square is drawn to represent a garden. One child is chosen to be Jack Frost. The other players represent leaves, flowers, or trees. They run, skip, or whirl any place inside the garden. When a player is touched by Jack Frost, she becomes frozen to the spot. The last player caught becomes Jack Frost for the next game.

Bowling

Indian clubs are placed in a three-foot circle, or if there are more then five clubs, they are set up in a triangle formation. Fifteen feet from the Indian clubs a line is drawn behind which the players stand in single file. Each child in turn rolls a ball (soccer ball, playground ball, 16-inch soft ball, or volleyball) towards the Indian clubs and attempts to knock them over. For every Indian club knocked over, a point is scored for that child. The Indian clubs are then set up for the next player.

Pass the Cap

The teams line up in file formation. All teams have an equal number of players. Each player has a ruler in his right hand. The first player has a ruler and a cap or hat. On a signal, the first player in line places his right arm over his shoulder, holding the cap on the ruler. The second player, using only the ruler, takes the cap from the first player and passes his arm over his right shoulder in such a way that the third player, using his ruler, may take the cap. When the last player receives the cap, he comes to the front of the line. The first team to complete the circuit is declared the winner.

Hint:
- If a player drops a cap, he must recover it by using the ruler only and not his hands or feet.

Eraser Tag

Two children are given blackboard erasers which they put on their heads. One is chased by the other. The chaser tries to catch the runner at the same time keeping the eraser on his head. After the eraser falls off either player's head, another player takes his place. When a runner is caught, a new player becomes the chaser.

Additional Comments:
- This game should not be played when there is a possibility of any children in the group having head lice.

Freight Train Tag

All of the players but one form groups of three, one behind the other, with their arms locked around the waist of the person ahead—each group of three composes a freight train. The odd player is IT and attempts to hook onto the end of any freight train. When he succeeds in doing this, the player at the head of the group becomes IT.

Pass the Fox

Players sit in a circle. An article (representing the fox) is passed rapidly from player to player. At a clap of the hand or if music is used, when the music stops for a moment, the object is passed in the opposite direction. Whoever drops or fumbles the object, must either pay a forfeit or go to the center of the circle. A forfeit can be any task or penalty—sing a song, run a lap, do a push-up. Forfeit is used as opposed to penalty with the intent that the word *forfeit* has a more neutral reference and can be anything the group decides. Music with a quick tempo helps to keep the game moving.

One-Legged Chicken

This game is played with small blocks of wood, beanbags, or stones. These are placed in straight rows of five to fifteen each, with intervals of about 10 inches between them. The players are divided into groups numbering from five to 10 each, and line up as for a relay race, each before one row of blocks.

The game is played in the same way by each row of players, and while the game may be competitive between the different groups in its original form, it is for one group only. The first player in a group represents a one-legged chicken and hops on one foot over each bag until the end of the line of bags has been reached. The last bag is then kicked away by the "lame" (lifted) foot, after which it must be picked up and carried back over the same route to the first end of the line. Then the same player hops back on the opposite foot, kicks away a second bag, picks it up, returns, and so on until he fails. Only one foot may touch the ground at a time, and may touch it but once in each space between the bags. No bag may be touched except the one at the end of the line, which is afterward picked up, and this must be secured without putting the lame foot upon the ground.

When the chicken infringes any of these rules, he must at once give place to another. The winner is the player who has picked up the greatest number of bags at the end of the game.

Cat and Mice

One player is chosen to be the cat, and hides behind or under a table or desk. After the cat is hidden, the leader beckons to five or six other players, who creep softly up to the table, and when all are assembled, scratch on it with their fingers to represent the nibbling of mice. As soon as the cat hears this, she scrambles out from under the table and gives chase to the mice, who may save themselves only by getting back to their "holes" (seats). If a mouse is caught, the cat changes places with him for the next round of the game. If no mouse is caught, the same cat may continue or the leader may choose another. A different group of mice should be chosen each time so as to give all the players an opportunity to join the game.

Hopscotch

Each player throws a pebble into Square 1 (see illustration), hops on one foot, picks up the pebble and hops back. The pebble then is thrown into Square 2, the player hops on one foot into Square 1, straddles Squares 2 and 3, picks up the pebble, puts weight on his left foot, and hops into Square 1 and out. The player may continue until the pebble fails to land in the proper square or he steps on a line or puts a foot down when he should not. He hops on one foot into Squares 1, 4, 7, and 10 and straddles the lines to retrieve the pebble in Squares 2, 3, 5, 6, 8, and 9. To provide for more activity, the players may follow these instructions but hop to the end and back each time the pebble is thrown and then pick it up. The players pick up the pebble on the way back.

Catch the Ball

The players are in a circle formation. One person is in the middle. Each player including the person in the middle is given a number. The player in the middle is given a playground ball which he holds above his head. He then calls a number and drops the ball. The person whose number was called must catch the ball on the first bounce. If he doesn't, he stays in the middle and the game continues.

Additional Comments:
- A basketball may be used also. If players catch the ball too easily, the circle should be widened. The leader should teach the children to respond quickly to their number.

Carry and Fetch Relay

Teams are in relay formation as for a simple relay race. The first player in each team has a beanbag. Upon the signal to start, he carries the beanbag and places it inside a circle drawn on the floor or ground just in front of his team and beyond the goal line. He then runs back and touches the second player, who runs, picks up the beanbag and brings it back and gives it to the third player. The third player takes it back to the circle, returns, and touches the fourth player, who runs to the circle, gets the beanbag, and so on. The team whose players have all run and are back in their original places first wins the race.

Hopscotch

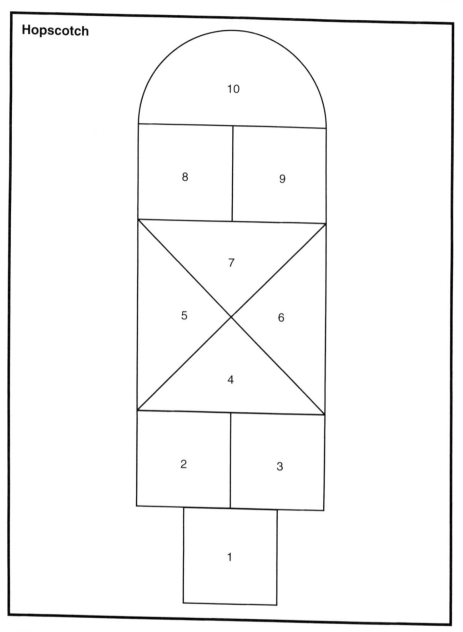

Additional Comments:
- The leader should watch for fouls (e.g., the beanbag must be inside the circle each time, the beanbag must be placed and not tossed, and the next player may not step forward to meet the runner). There are many fouls which the leader can and should enforce depending on the closeness of the race.

Circle Blind Swat

All but one of the players is arranged in a single circle, players facing in and holding hands. The extra player is IT and stands in the center of the circle. IT is blindfolded and has a swatter. At a signal, IT runs to swat one of the players of the circle. The circle may move to keep IT from swatting one of its members. The players, however, must retain their grasped hands. The chase continues until a player has been hit and then IT asks him three questions which this player must answer. The player may answer the questions in a disguised voice. IT may make one guess as to who the player is after each answer. If IT fails to guess correctly, he remains IT, returns to the center of the circle, and at a signal, the game continues. If he guesses correctly, the two players exchange places and the game continues.

Duck on the Rock

The throwing line is 20-feet long. The leader places a flat rock, brick, or a block of wood 40 feet in front of the line. Each member of the group gets a stone about the size of a fist and takes position at the throwing line. One of the players is IT and takes a position at the rock, placing his stone (duck) on the same. At a signal, the players on the line toss their ducks at the rock, attempting to dislodge the duck resting there. After tossing, players attempt to secure their rocks and return to the throwing line with it, without being tagged and ITs duck must be on the rock at the time of tagging to make a tag valid. Any player knocking the duck off of the rock gets a free passage back to the starting line. Any player tagged by IT displaces the old IT. The new IT places his own duck on the rock, and the old IT is given a free passage to the starting line.

Heads and Tails

Two parallel lines are established 60 feet apart. The group is divided into two teams of equal numbers and stand back-to-back four feet apart in the center of the field parallel to the baselines. The line each team faces is that team's baseline. One team is heads and the other is tails. At a signal, the leader tosses up a coin and calls the side that lands faceup. The side that is called runs for its baseline, attempting to get there before any player of the opposite team can tag them. Any player tagged by an opponent before he reaches his baseline must give his tagger a free ride back to his position in the center of the field. When all have crossed the baseline or have been tagged and carried, all return to their original positions, and the coin is tossed up again. In this manner the game continues.

Marching Bear Chase

A circle two feet in diameter is established in the center of the field of play. This is the "den." A line is established 40 feet from the den. This is the base. All of the players but one stands in a circle around the den. The extra player is the bear and he sits in the den. The bear announces any number up to 40. It may be 10, 17, 22, or 26. At a signal, the players forming the circle march forward around the circle at a normal marching rate. The bear counts their steps aloud as they march—one, two, three, four. On reaching the announced number, all break ranks and run for the base. At the same time the bear rises and gives chase, attempting to catch and hold one of them before reaching the base. Any player caught and held for five seconds becomes bear. If no one is caught the bear retains his office. In either case, the bear and other players return to their positions. The bear declares a new number (less than 40), the group marches about and the game continues as before.

Hot Rice

The players are scattered over the playing area. The leader establishes a base (a spot one-foot square in the center of the area). One player is IT. The leader gives him a bat and playground ball, and places him on the base. At a signal, IT

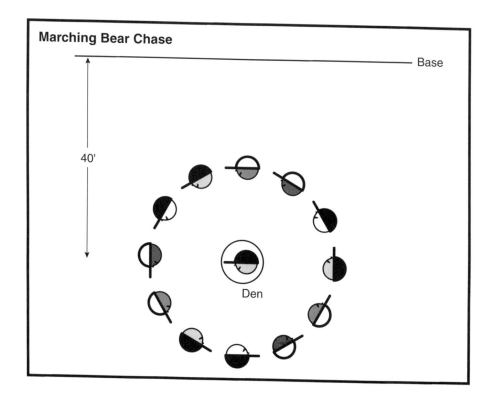

Marching Bear Chase

Base

40'

Den

bats the ball. The other players attempt to recover the ball as soon as possible; the player who secures it throws it at the batter. The batter either tries to bat it, avoid it, or use the bat to prevent it from hitting him. He must, however, keep one foot on the base. If the ball hits the batter, the player who threw it and the batter exchange places. To catch a batted ball the players may run about as they wish; the player who captures the ball, however, must throw it at once from the point where he captured it. Any player catching two fly balls off the bat also exchanges places with the batter. Each new batter restarts the game by batting the ball.

Move Down or up

The group is divided into two teams of equal number; they stand in parallel lines 25–50 feet apart, teams facing each other, players four feet apart. One of the players starts with a ball. At a signal, the player with the ball calls the name of one of the players of the opposite team and throws the ball to him. The throw may be (1) a roller, (2) a bouncer, (3) a straight pitch, or (4) a fly; the thrower has his choice. The player should make his throw so that it is fairly difficult to catch, but not too difficult. The player whose name is called attempts to catch it. If he misses the ball, he moves down one spot and exchanges places with the player on his right. The place of honor is to the right of the lines. Succeeding or failing, the player secures the ball and, calling a name of one of the players on the opposite line, throws it to him. This player moves up one, or moves down one according to whether he catches the ball. This player calls the name of a player of the opposite side and throws the ball, and so forth in this manner, the game continues.

Rattlesnake

All but three members of the group are in a circle 20 feet in diameter, players facing in. Of the three selected players one is the snake and has a can with pebbles in it or a small bell. The other two players are blindfolded—these are the hunters. The snake and the hunters stand in separate positions inside of the circle. At a signal, the two hunters call, "Rattle, snake," whereupon the snake rattles the can. Upon hearing the rattle, both of the blindfolded players attempt to catch the snake. The snake attempts to evade the hunters. Either of the blindfolded players may at any time ask the snake to rattle and the snake must respond to every request. The chase continues until the snake is caught. When the snake is caught, he retires to the circle, the hunter who caught him becomes the snake, and a new hunter is appointed. At a signal, the game continues.

Shuttlecock Target Toss

The leader will draw the target as shown in the illustration on the floor or ground. From a line 15 or more feet distant the players take turns in throwing a shuttlecock (or beanbag), endeavoring to make it fall into the scoring area.

Swat to the Right

All but one member of the group is in a circle—players standing shoulder-to-shoulder, facing in. The players place their hands behind their backs. The extra player has a swatter and stands outside the circle. At a signal, the player having the swatter runs outside the circle, and at his discretion places the swatter in the hands of another. The player receiving it immediately hits (taps) the player on his right. The player hit runs to the right around the circle until he is back at his starting position. The player who first carried the swatter drops into the position vacated by the player to whom he has passed the swatter. The player with the swatter follows the runner, hitting him with it as often as he can until he is back in position. The player with the swatter then runs on and places the swatter in some other player's hands and drops into that player's position as that player leaves. In this manner the game continues.

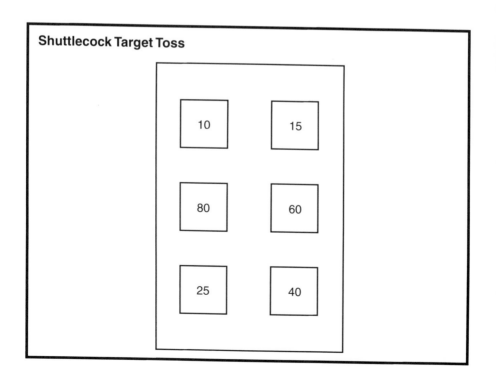

Shuttlecock Target Toss

Target Pitch

Two stakes or marks or small objects are placed 60 feet apart. Each player gets a beanbag. Alternatively each may remove one shoe. Each player marks the object with his initials—using chalk, ink, or pencil. All of the players stand in a line behind one stake. The players are numbered consecutively. At a signal, the first player throws his object at the other stake, the second follows, and then the third. All throws must be underhand. When all have thrown, the one having his object nearest the stake scores one point. All pick up their objects, arrange themselves in a line behind the stake and at a signal, starting with the second player, all throw in turn at the first stake. The player who threw first previously throws last. This continues until all have thrown first. The player with the highest score wins.

Touch and Win

Two parallel lines are drawn 50 feet apart. The group is divided into two teams of equal numbers and placed on opposite baselines. The players stand at normal intervals, facing in. At a signal, the player on the right of Team A runs forward. All of the players of Team B stretch one of their hands forward on the first and same signal. The runner touches any of the outstretched hands and then races back to his line. The player struck chases the runner, attempting to tag him before he reaches the baseline. The player who succeeds in his efforts takes the other player as his prisoner and places him behind his own baseline. The play is reversed. At a signal, the first player to the right of Team B runs forward and repeats the efforts of the first runner. This continues with players running alternately from each side and touching any member of the opposing team. Each player keeps his own prisoners behind him. If any player who has prisoners is made a prisoner himself, the prisoners he had are released and returned to their original positions. The game continues until all have run forward. The team having the most prisoners at the conclusion wins.

Balloon Blow

Each player has a balloon and a straw. The players race to a goal line propelling their balloons by blowing through the straws.

Packing Kendra's Schoolbag

(This is a quiet game for a rest period.) One player starts the game by saying, "I am packing Kendra's schoolbag, and I shall put in some apples." The next one says, "I am packing Kendra's schoolbag, she has apples, and I shall put in a book." This continues around the circle, each player naming all that has been packed and adding something beginning with the next letter of the alphabet.

Center Catch Ball

All the players but one stand in a circle. The odd player stands in the center and tries to catch the ball, which is tossed rapidly from one player to another. If he succeeds in catching it, he changes places with the person who last touched it. If he touches the ball while another player holds it or while it is in the air, the player responsible must change places with him and go into the center.

Games for the
Middle Grades

Animal Relays

Relays may be varied by the players progressing to the goal and back in the manner of some animal walk. Variations may be:

1. Donkey walk, traveling on all fours to the goal and imitating the donkey's kick and bray;
2. Crab walk, walking on all fours and with the face up;
3. Bear walk, walking on all fours with feet going outside the hands; and
4. Duck walk, walking on two feet in squat position.

Additional Comments:
- Other animal walks which have already been used as stunts may be used. Difficult stunts should be learned first before they are used in a relay.
- The leader should not use stunts which involve walking on the hands on the playground unless the surface is soft and clean.
- Suggestions for teaching relays are included with the description of Simple Relays.

Fly Swatter

The players stand in a circle formation with their hands behind their backs. A rolled newspaper is used as a fly swatter. The player who is IT has the fly swatter and is outside of the circle formed by the other players. He goes around the outside of the circle and places the fly swatter in the hands of any one of the players. Upon receiving the fly swatter, the player begins to chase the player who is on his right, swatting at him with the fly swatter; both run counter-clockwise around the circle until the runner returns to his place in the circle.

The one with the fly swatter is then IT and places the fly swatter in the hands of another player and the game continues. The player who is IT always steps into the circle vacated by the player to whom he gave the swatter.

Additional Comments:
- The leader should be prepared with more than one fly swatter as the fly swatter will tear easily. A knotted towel may be used as a swatter.
- The leader should *insist* that hits must be below the shoulders and not too hard.

Commando

One player is IT and he is inside a circle formed by six to eight players who have their hands joined. The players in the circle try to prevent IT from breaking through the circle and thus freeing himself. He may break through by crawling under or over the joined hands, by breaking the hand holds of the players or by any means he may devise. Whenever IT breaks through the circle, the players chase him. The player who first tags him is IT for the repetition of the game.

Additional Comments:
- The leader should group players of nearly equal size and strength together.

Cross Tag

After the players have scattered over the play area, the leader designates the player who is to be IT and the one who is to be the runner. The player who is IT chases the runner, attempting to tag him. The runner is safe only when someone crosses between him and the chaser. The player who crosses between them becomes the runner, and when more than one player crosses, the player nearest to IT is the runner. When IT is successful in tagging a runner, he becomes the runner and the tagged player becomes IT. Players may cross voluntarily to assist the runner; or a player may be forced to cross between the two as the runner runs around a player so that he comes between them.

Additional Comments:
- The leader may need to stop the game for explanation as the children play the game for the first time. The leader may start with only six or seven players so that the pattern of crossing is clearer.
- Often it is difficult to succeed in tagging. The leader should watch the child who is IT and protect him from overfatigue by selecting another player to be IT.

- The leader should encourage voluntary assistance to the runner as the children learn to play the game. The fun in the game lies in this element.

Dumbbell Tag

The players are scattered over the play area. One player is selected to be the runner; he is given a dumbbell. To start the game, the leader calls the name of the player who is to be the chaser of IT. He gives chase. The player who has the dumbbell may, at any time, give it to another player who, upon receiving it, becomes the runner. No one can refuse to take the dumbbell when it is handed to him. If IT tags a player having the dumbbell, that player becomes IT after giving the dumbbell to another player. He allows that player a fair chance to get started before he chases him.

Additional Comments:
- Any object which is easy to handle, such as a knotted towel, may be used in place of a dumbbell.
- The leader should prohibit throwing the dumbbell; the runner must hand the dumbbell to another player.

Four Square

The playing area is a square approximately eight feet on each side (chalk may be used on a sidewalk or driveway or playground, masking tape on an indoor floor). The large square is divided into four evenly divided squares. Each square is marked 1, 2, 3, or 4. One player stands on the outside of each square. The player at Square 1, serves by dropping a playground ball and with an under-hand motion hits it to any of the other squares. The player at that square must let the ball bounce only once before hitting the ball (underhand motion) to any other square, not his own. This continues until (1) the receiving player fails to return the ball, (2) the person hitting the ball fails to hit another square, or (3) the ball bounces more than once in a square. The person making the error leaves his square and goes to the end of the line. The player behind then moves up to that person's square. The person who is at Square 1 serves again. The person in Square 4 receives one point for each play he stays in Square 4. The winner is the person who has the most points at the end of the game (time limit).

Note:
- Balls landing on a line counts.
- Each player is responsible for the internal line to his right.
- Each player must keep at least one foot outside his square at all times (he may reach forward with one foot inside his square to reach a ball).

- A player who has one foot inside his square and is hit in that foot by the ball before it bounces is out. However, if he is standing completely outside his square and an errant ball hit by another hits him directly before it bounces, then the person hitting the ball is out.

Four Trips

Teams of three players are chosen and the players in each team are numbered One, Two, and Three. Number Ones are the captains of the teams and they each stand in one of the circles of bases drawn equidistant from side-to-side across the center of the play area. Number Twos are with their captains on bases in a line across one end of the play area and 20 feet from the center. Number Threes are on similar bases at the opposite end and 20 feet from the center. The ball is thrown in trips, and the team first completing four trips wins.

A trip is when the captain throws the ball to Number Two, who throws it to Number Three, and Number Three throws the ball back to the captain. The captain must call the number of the completed trip each time he catches the ball. The ball must be thrown while the thrower has contact with the base (at least one foot on the base). If the ball is caught by a player off of his base, the player must return to his base to make the throw.

A signal from the leader starts the first throws from the captains simultaneously.

Four Trips

Player 2		Captain or Player 1		Player 3
2A	Team A	1A		3A
2B	Team B	1B		3B
2C	Team C	1C		3C
2D	Team D	1D		3D
2E	Team E	1E		3E

Additional Comments:
- The type of ball used (e.g., softball, football, volleyball, or basketball) as well as the distance between the bases will depend upon players' abilities and seasonal interests. The leader should coach the players to throw according to the type of ball used and the distance desired.
- The game may be changed to Six Trips, Ten Trips, or any other number according to the types of throws and the skills of the players.

Goal Ball

Goal Ball is played with a junior football, and the playing field, 60 or more feet long, is marked with side boundary lines, goal lines, a center line, and two goal areas. From six to nine players form each of two teams. About one third of the players on each team are goalies; the remainder are fielders. The goalies stand inside the goal area just back of the opponent's field area, and the fielders are scattered over the team's field area.

A point is scored when a pass is completed from a fielder to one of his goalies while the goalies has at least one foot in his goal area. The game is started, on a signal from the referee, by a goalie from either team selected by chance. He attempts to pass the ball from within his goal area to another fielder or tries to score by passing directly to one of his goalies. Whenever a pass is intercepted by an opposing goalie, the play continues. A fielder may pass either to a goalie or to another fielder at any time but he must pass the ball from

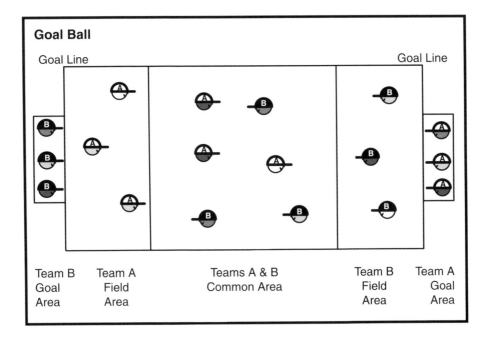

the spot where he caught it, and he cannot hold the ball more than three seconds. A fielder cannot step into the goal area or into the opponent's field area.

Whenever the ball goes out of bounds over the sidelines, a nearby player recovers the ball, brings it just inside the boundary line at the point where it went out, and plays it from there. If a ball goes over a goal line or is caught by a goalie while he is outside of his goal area, the ball is dead; it is put into play from inside the goal area at the opposite end of the field by a goalie and on a signal from the referee.

The penalty for any violation of the rules, unless the opponents score before the penalty is called, is a pass, upon a signal from the referee, from a goalie of the opposing team.

After a point is scored, the ball is put into play by a goalie of the team scored against. Play is continued through two five-minute halves with a three-minute rest between halves. The team that scores the most points during the playing period wins the game. The size of the field will depend upon the number of players and the abilities of the players.

Additional Comments:
- Note that Goal Ball is similar to End Ball. The primary differences include the type of ball used, the sizes of the teams, the goal areas, and the methods of putting the ball into play at the start of the games and during the play.

Hindoo Tag

The players are scattered over a limited playing area. One is chosen as IT and he attempts to tag another player. The players are safe when in the "hindoo" position; that is, on their knees with their forehead resting on their hands on the floor.

Additional Comments:
- The leader should teach the children how to fall quickly and safely into the hindoo position before playing the game. He should teach them to stoop down, take the body weight on the hands with the fingers pointed in and elbows bending, and then gently lower the knees to the floor.
- The leader should encourage the players to move about continuously.
- This game only should be played on a gymnasium floor or on a grassy playground.

Over and Under Relay

Players are in a relay formation (see Simple Relay). The first player in each file has a ball. At the signal to start, the first player passes the ball over his head to the second player, who passes it between his legs to the third. The ball is passed "over and under" the whole length of the file. The last player, upon receiving the ball, runs forward to the front of his file and starts the ball again. This is continued until the file is back in its original lineup with the ball in the hands of the original first player. The file finishing first wins.

The ball is always started over the head of the player at the front of the file. The ball is passed or handed to the next player; it is not thrown.

Numbers Change

All players are given a number and one is selected to be IT. The players stand in a circle with IT in the center. He calls any two numbers. The players whose numbers he calls must exchange places while the player who is IT attempts to get one of their places in the circle. The player who is left without a place is IT for the next time and he calls the two numbers for the next change.

Additional Comments:
- The leader should assign the players their numbers by asking them to count off as they stand in the circle; and then mix up the players after they receive their numbers so that the numbers do not occur in consecutive order in the circle.
- The circle should be kept large by spreading the players out from the center and having 10 to 15 players in each circle.
- The leader should be sure that the player who calls the numbers remains in the center of the circle until he has called both numbers.

Variations:
- The player in the center is blindfolded and he tries to tag one of the players as they change places. A player who is tagged becomes IT.

Snake Catch

The players are scattered over the playing area. One player is appointed as the snake catcher. He is given a rope about six-feet long. Upon a signal, he runs over the playing area dragging the free end of the rope on the ground. The other players try to catch the rope in their hands. Anyone catching it becomes the snake catcher. In attempting to catch the rope, the players cannot step on it. The snake catcher must drag one end of the rope on the floor or ground, and he must stop as soon as a player catches the rope; otherwise, the hands of the catcher may be burned as the rope is pulled through them.

Additional Comments:
- The leader should be sure that the snake catcher drags the rope on the floor or ground, and that he stops immediately when a catch is made.

Simon Says

One player is selected as the leader. He stands in the front of the other players standing in rows facing the leader. The leader gives commands, some of which are prefaced by "Simon says," and some of which are not. The players must do everything commanded which is preceded by "Simon says;" but they must not obey a command which is not preceded by "Simon says." Any player who makes a mistake must sit down in his seat if the leader sees the error and calls his name. After the leader has caught three players making errors, another leader is selected, the three players get into the game again, and the game starts again with the new leader giving commands.

Additional Comments:
- The leader should select an alert child to be the leader, otherwise, the game may move slowly and be uninteresting.
- The leader should not keep the children who "miss" out of the game too long.
- The leader may suggest, when necessary, commands such as jump rope, saw wood, skip in place, stretch, nod head, bend forward, and turn around.

Sardine

Sardine is a hide-and-seek game. It differs from the usual Hide-and-Seek in that the player who is IT hides and all of the other players set out to find him. He is given time to hide and then, after an established period of time, the others start to hunt for him. Any players finding him must hide with him. The last one finding the hiding place is IT for the next game. If there is not room for all of the players to hide in the hiding place, they must wait within sight of the hiding place until all have found the original hider.

Additional Comments:
- The leader should caution players to remain quiet after they have found the hider in order not to give away the hiding place. Suggestions for hiding games are included with the description of Hide-and-Seek.

Second Base Ball

This game is played by two teams, and with a playground ball. An elongated base encloses the second base of the softball diamond. The players of the at-bat team kick the ball placed on the home plate, run to second base, and run back to home plate. If a player tags the home plate before he is put out, he scores one point for his team; he is out if the ball which he kicked is caught by an opponent before it hits the ground, or if he is hit below the waist by a ball held or thrown by a fielder. Fielders must throw the ball from where it was caught; they cannot hold the ball longer than three seconds; and they cannot run with the ball.

The players on each team, are numbered for "batting" order before the game is started. The game starts with one team in the field and the other team at bat. When three outs are called against the team at bat, the teams change positions and the team in the field comes in, while the team that was kicking goes out in the field.

Both teams play an equal number of turns at bat and in the field, or for an established number of innings. The team that scores more points during the playing time wins the game.

Scoring may be changed and one point awarded for each runner reaching second base and for each runner reaching home plate safely. The long base permits several runners to await the run into home plate and the players are allowed to sit on second base; however, a runner can only run after a ball is kicked and if he leaves second base, he must continue his run to the home plate.

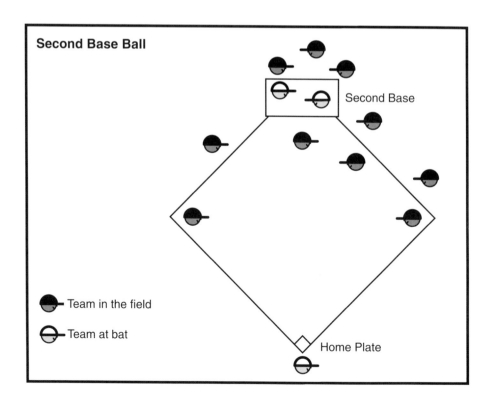

Second Base Ball

Second Base

Team in the field

Team at bat

Home Plate

Additional Comments:
- The leader should teach quick and accurate passing, and teach the players to kick with the toe of the foot to get distance.
- The leader may incorporate softball rules into the game when the players are able to follow them.
- If played in an indoor gym, the kickers may kick the ball anywhere. In other words, there would be no traditional foul balls.
- The leader should be aware of safety hazards and those unsafe areas (ceiling lights, perhaps equipment stored in a corner) could be out-of-bounds and/or result in an automatic out. He or she should stress to the players the reason for safety.

Teacher Ball Relay

This game is played as a relay with two or more equal teams of approximately six players each competing. Each of the players assumes the position of the leader during one round of the relay. Whenever a ball is missed, the player missing the catch recovers the ball and returns to his playing position to toss the ball in. Lines are marked indicating the playing position of the leader and the players for each team.

The relay starts on a signal and the ball is tossed from the leader to players as in Teacher Ball. When the player at the foot of the line receives the ball, he runs with the ball to the leader's position, the former leader runs to the position at the head of the line, and the next round continues with the new leader. This is repeated until each player on the team has played the leader's position and the original leader is back in his first position. The team that finishes first wins the relay.

Team Dodge Ball

Team Dodge Ball is played as Simple Dodge Ball except that the players form two equal teams. One team is in a circle and it attempts to hit, or put out, the players of the other team who are inside the circle. The game is played from one to two minutes and the number of players put out is counted. The teams change places and play again for the same length of time. The team wins which has put out more of the opposing team in the given playing time. Players who are put out stay out of the game until the teams change places. It may be necessary to mark a circle on the ground or floor and require players to remain outside of the circle as they throw.

Team Relay

The players stand in a relay formation and each file represents a team. The leader gives commands to touch materials or colors. All players respond to the command and return to the original formation with each file in its own place. The team that is back in its formation first scores one point. The team that wins five points first wins the game.

Commands given might be touch brick, touch red, touch iron, touch wood, or touch green.

Additional Comments:
- The players should get in their own files and in their place on the floor, but do not need to get in their original places in their file.
- The leader should know his area and have commands in mind before starting the game. The commands must fit the place and must give each team a chance to win.

Ten Steps

Ten steps is played as Red Light, Green Light except that the players start from the goal line, proceed away from the player who is IT, and then hide as soon as they are out of sight. After all are out of sight, the player who is IT sets out to find them. Each child tries to be the last one found. Those who are found return to the goal and wait for the others to be found.

Three Deep

One player is chosen as the runner and another as IT. The remaining players stand in a double circle with partners standing one in front of the other and facing the center of the circle. The one who is IT chases the runner, who is safe by stepping in front of any couple in the circle, whereupon the outside player of that couple immediately becomes the runner and the game continues. Whenever a runner is tagged, he becomes IT and the player who tagged him becomes the runner.

Additional Comments:
- Because it is rather easy for the runner to save himself, the one who is IT may have difficulty in tagging anyone and may be IT for too long. The leader should watch for this as it makes the game drag and that particular child may become fatigued. He should allow someone to take his place.
- The players may not cut across the circle. They must go around the outside of the circle.

Variations:
- When a runner steps in front of a couple, the outside player becomes the chaser and the former chaser immediately becomes the runner.

- Partners face each other. The runner then stops in between two players to save himself. The one he faces becomes his partner and the one to whom he turns his back becomes the runner.

Turtle Tag

Turtle Tag is played as a simple tag game except that the players are safe when on their backs with "all fours" up (hands and feet must be off the floor).

Additional Comments:
- The leader should teach the players how to fall safely into the safety position: stoop down, take weight on hands with fingers pointing in and elbows bending, and pushing with the hands, roll over onto the hips, shoulder, and back. The players should practice this as a skill before putting it into the game.

Opposites

The group is arranged in a circle, players standing three feet apart, facing in. Each of the players raises both hands sideward and holds opposite corners of a handkerchief with his neighbors. The leader then calls, "Let go," "Hold fast," "Tight," "Loose," and so on. The players should respond opposite to the commands, letting the handkerchief fall to the floor on such commands as "Hold fast" and "Tight" and holding it on such commands as "Drop it," "Loose," and "Let go." When the handkerchief is on the floor, the leader says, "Let it lie," while the players respond opposite to this commands also. Each false move on the part of a player scores a dud for him. This continues until one player has three duds. This player must pay a forfeit.

Poison Seat

The contestants sit in their seats. The leader places a book on each seat that is empty and also places a book on one seat that is occupied. At a signal, all of the contestants change seats, attempting to get one that does not hold a book. Seats holding books are poisoned and cannot be occupied. The child left without a seat is eliminated and takes position in front of the room. The leader puts a book on another occupied seat. At a signal, all change again. The child left without a seat is eliminated as before. In this manner, play continues until all but two have been eliminated. These are the winners.

Cat and Dog

Prior to the game, the leader should draw and cut out several bones from paper. He will hide the bones around the room. The players number off and one group is dogs and the other group, cats. Each side then chooses a leader. At a blast from the whistle, all start to look for the bones. When anyone sights a bone, he cannot pick it up, but must stand in front of it and give the tribal signal—if a cat, he must meow; if a dog, bark—until the leader of that team comes and picks up the bone. At the end of a given time, the team that has the most bones collected wins.

Jellybean Hunt

The group is divided into two or more teams, each with a captain, and each member of each team is given a name of an animal. One person hides jelly-beans, and members of each team hunt for them. When they find a jellybean, they make a noise like the animal they are pretending to be and the captain of the team then picks up the jellybean. The captain is the only one who can pick up jellybeans. The team with the most jellybeans wins.

Two Division Dodge Ball

Two Division Dodge Ball is played with two teams in adjacent courts playing against each other by trying to put out the opposing players at the same time. A player is put out when he is hit below the waist by a ball thrown by an opponent, or if a player catches a ball thrown by an opponent. The ball is "dead" and cannot put out a player after it has hit one player, touched the floor, or gone outside the playing area. When a ball goes outside the boundary lines of the court, it is recovered by a nearby player, who brings it just inside the boundary line and puts it in play.

When a player is put out, he leaves the court for the time remaining in that playing period. The game is over when one team eliminates all the players from the opposing team. A time limit may also be used to end a game.

Additional Comments:
- Several playground balls may be used at once.
- Suggestions are included with the description of Simple Dodge Ball.
- The leader may score the number of players put out for both teams at the end of each playing period; add these after the third period to determine the winner.

Star Wars Dodge Ball

One player from each team is designated as Obi-Wan. Obi-Wan holds a sword (plastic Wiffle ball bat). The game is over when the opposing Obi-Wan is hit with a ball. The other team members act as guards and must protect their Obi-Wan and must sacrifice themselves as necessary. If a guard is hit by a ball, or if his thrown ball is caught by an opposing guard (see Two Division Dodge Ball), he sits down in the exact spot where he got hit or where he threw the ball. Guards reenter the game when Obi-Wan taps them on the shoulder with his sword.

Generic Dodge Ball

Generic Dodge Ball is played similar to Two Division Dodge Ball, but played as an individual instead of a team game. Everyone is on his own. The game is started in a circle formation. The leader (or winner of the previous game), tosses a playground ball into the air. Players either scatter or attempt to retrieve the ball. Once a player retrieves the ball, she can take only three steps in any direction before throwing the ball at another player. If the ball strikes another player, then that player is eliminated from the game and becomes a spectator. However, if he catches the ball, then the player who threw the ball is eliminated. The game continues until all but one player is eliminated.

Dodge Ball Variations

There are numerous variations to Generic Dodge Ball. The leader and players may use their imagination to make their own variations. The following are several that have been tried:

- *Rotation Dodge Ball:* Same as Generic Dodge Ball, however, in this game if a player gets hit, or if someone catches the ball he threw, instead of being eliminated, he sits down in the exact spot where he got hit (or someone caught his ball). If in the process of the continuing game, he can touch the ball (staying in the seated position), he is back in the game. This can occur multiple times. The game is over when every player except one is seated. This game is good for smaller groups.
- *Double Rotation Dodge Ball:* Same as Rotation Dodge Ball, except if a player gets hit (or someone catches his ball) a second time, then he is eliminated. The game ends when either everyone is seated or eliminated.
- *Silent Dodge Ball:* Same as Generic, Rotation, and Double Rotation Dodge Ball, except this game is played silently. If a player talks or laughs, he is out as if he got hit. This variation tends to calm the group down if after several other games they are getting loud.
- *Opposite Hand Throw Dodge Ball:* Players must throw with their non-dominant hand. Since they will not be able to throw with the same accuracy or strength, the players may take five steps instead of three.
- *One-Leg Throw Dodge Ball:* Players must throw standing on one leg.

- *Candy Bar Dodge Ball:* Players must name a candy bar before throwing the ball. No repeats of candy bars are allowed. If a player forgets to name a candy bar and hits another player, it doesn't count.
- *Apology Dodge Ball:* This is dodge ball with manners. When a player throws the ball and legally hits another player, the player who threw the ball *must* say, "Sorry about that." The hit player will respond, "That's all right," or "Nice shot." If the thrower's ball is caught, the responses are, "Nice catch," and, "Thanks!"

Note:
- The purpose of several of these variations is an attempt to reduce the intensity which this game can produce. By apologizing, remaining silent, or saying a candy bar's name, the attempt is made to laugh and have fun with this popular game.

Yards off

A goal such as a post, tree, or the wall of a building is chosen. The players gather around the goal. The leader, throwing a stick away from the goal, calls the name of a player. That player is IT and he recovers the stick and stands it against the goal while the other players run and hide. He seeks the hiders as soon as he places the stick against the goal. Any player seen by IT must return to the goal and throw the stick away from the goal without being seen by the player who was IT. This frees all the prisoners, and they hide again. IT may not seek other players until he has placed the stick back against the goal. The last player caught may be the thrower of the next game.

Additional Comments:
- Suggestions for teaching hiding games are described with Hide-and-Seek.
- A stick, an Indian club, or any other suitable object may be used.

Variations:
- The leader may mark a circle on the ground for the goal and use a block of wood instead of the stick. The block is kicked instead of thrown.

How Many Can You Remember?

The leader places 20 or 30 objects on a table. Everyone looks at them for two or three minutes. Then they are covered. The winner is the person writing down the greatest number of correct objects.

Ankle Tag

This game is played like a simple tag game, except that a player is "safe" from tagging if he has hold of another player's ankle or ankles. The player whose ankle is held, however, is vulnerable to tagging unless he has hold of some other player's ankle. This may be the player holding his own, or it may be another's.

Foot Grab

Two teams of equal number face each other about 20 feet apart. The leader calls one player from each team. These players come to the center of the play area and the first player to grab the foot of his opponent scores a point for his team. These players return and the leader calls two more players as the game continues.

Mass Soccer

A goal, the approximate width of a soccer goal, is marked at each end of the playing field. The leader will divide the players into two equal teams and assign each to one half of the field. He will assign four members of each team to guard the goal. The object for each team is to kick the ball through the opponent's goal and at the same time to prevent balls from being kicked through its own goal.

The leader will start the game by placing all balls in the center of the field. At a signal, the players rush forward and kick the balls. The ball may not be touched with the hands except by the guards. The guards may catch and throw a ball when in the area of the goal.

One point is scored for every ball kicked through the goal.

Line Soccer

(This game is best played indoors, in a gym.) Goal lines are marked off at both ends of the gym. The leader will divide the players into two equal teams and assign each player on each team a number. (Both teams will have a Number 1, 2, 3, 4, and so on.) The leader calls out a number and tosses a soccer ball at midfield. The players whose number was called become the soccer players and duel each other to score a goal. The others become the goalies. The object is for one of the players to score a goal on the opposing team (kick the ball past the goalies and below the shoulder). Once this occurs, the players whose numbers were called go back to their teams and the leader calls another number and play continues.

Additional Comments:
- The leader should make sure that all players have the opportunity to be a soccer player an equal number of times.
- As a variation, the leader may call out more than one number at a time, e.g. "numbers two and four." Or, if play becomes too slow, the leader may call an additional number to help out.
- Goalies can use their hands and throw the ball to their teammates.

Jungle Jim

Twelve children form a hollow square or circle. The leader winds in and out of the square or circle tapping children who identify themselves as certain animals or birds. As each child is tapped, he follows the leader in a snakelike line until the entire group is drawn into the square or circle. The group sings, "We Went to the Animal Fair." The leader then calls upon each child to give an imitation of the animal he represents. The child who gives the best imitation becomes the next leader.

Tug of War

Players are divided into two teams, and a line is drawn through the center of the field. Each team lines up in a single file with the first player on each team facing across the center line. If a rope is used, the players grasp it tightly. If not, each player places his arms around the player in front of him and the two players at the center grasp each others' wrists. The first team to pull the other over the center line wins. If a line breaks, the players can either re-form at that position, or a winner can be declared. The best two out of three wins the match.

Circle Tug

A circle four feet in diameter is drawn on the playing area. The players are arranged in a ring about the circle, players standing shoulder-to-shoulder and facing in. Each player puts his arms about the shoulders of the two adjoining players. At a signal, each player attempts to draw the other players into the circle. Players forced to step inside of the circle are eliminated and withdraw from the ring. After a player withdraws, the circle is re-formed and at a signal, the game is restarted. In case the ring of players becomes broken, the game is halted, and players rejoin and the game is restarted, as in the beginning. The game continues until only one player is left. When the number of players gets so small they cannot encompass the circle, the ring of players is formed at one side of the circle, and again each attempts to eliminate the others.

Cut the Cake

Players form a circle. The player who is IT goes in the center and cuts the cake by touching the hands of two players in the circle. The two players run in opposite directions around the circle and back to their places. IT steps into one of the vacancies and stays there. Whoever of the two running around the circle gets back to the other vacancy first, leaves the other one to be IT. IT then cuts the cake.

Bronco Tag

Players stand in a circle, in groups of three, one behind the other, the second clasping the first, and the third clasping the second around the waist. The first of each group of three represents the head of the bronco, the second the body, the third the tail. Two players are chosen to be the runner and the chaser. The runner, to avoid being caught, tries to catch hold of the tail of the bronco, but the bronco whirls away from him and tries to keep him off by dodging first one way and then another. If he should succeed in getting hold of the bronco, the player who is the head must then be the runner. And so the game continues. If the chaser tags the runner before he catches hold of a bronco's tail, then the runner becomes the chaser and must try to tag him back.

Four All Around

Players stand in files or rows of four each, facing the center of a circle, like the spokes of a wheel. One player is selected to be IT and stands outside, either back of a file or between two files.

IT runs around the circle and tags the outside player of one file. This player passes the tag to the one ahead of him, and so on until the tag reaches the first player of the group who says, "Go." This is the signal for the file to separate and run, in any direction, around the outside of the circle, until the original place of the file is reached. In the meantime, IT continues running around the circle until he reaches the position of the disbanded file. The first four of the five runners who re-forms the file are safe; the fifth or odd player is IT and starts the next game as before.

Leapfrog

The leader will arrange the players in single file formation in several groups of approximately 10 in each group, placing all of the boys together and all of the girls together. The leader will assign one player from each group to a position about 10 feet in front of his or her line. The distance may be shortened if space is limited. This player should bend double and standing with either his or her

Four All Around

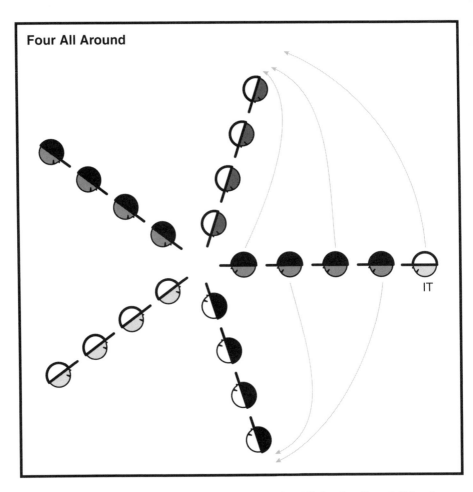

back or side towards the line, should make a "back" for the first child to jump. The object of the game is for each player in turn to run forward, place his or her hands on the player who is making the back, vault over him or her, run forward, and make a back. If there is more than one back, he or she vaults each in turn. The game starts at a signal or whenever the first back is ready.

Additional Comments:
- If there is an extra large group, multiple leapers may be used to keep the game moving.

Variations:
- The game may be made more difficult by having the backs close together, so that there is no chance for a run between vaults.

Lover's Golf

Equipment: A large heart two feet in diameter, marked or sketched on a piece of wallboard. Upon this large heart are drawn or pasted eight red hearts and one black heart three to six inches wide (see illustration). Six or twelve darts are also required.

Game: The object of the game is to get around the course from number one to number eight in the fewest number of shots. Each player may throw three darts before his turn is over. If he makes a "heart in one," he may shoot until he misses. Anyone hitting the black heart (refusal) must start over.

High Windows

All of the players but one join hands in a circle. The odd player in the center (IT) runs around on the inside of the circle and touches one of the players with a wisp of grass, if the game is played out-of-doors, or tags him if played indoors. Both players then run out of the circle, the object being for the player who was tagged to catch IT before he can run three times around the outside of the ring. As IT completes his third time around, the players in the circle cry,

Lover's Golf

1. Single blessedness
2. Acquaintance
3. Friendship
4. Love
5. Courtship
6. Proposal
7. Engagement
8. Marriage
9. *Refusal*

"High windows," and raise their clasped hands to let both of the players inside the circle. Should IT succeed in entering the circle without being tagged, he joins the circle and the chaser becomes IT in the center. Should the chaser tag IT before he can circle the ring three times and dodge inside, the chaser returns to the circle, and IT goes again into the center.

It is permissible to vary the chase by running away from the immediate vicinity of the circle. Should the chase then become too long, the circle players may call, "High windows," as a signal for the runners to come in. This call is made at the discretion of a leader.

Merry-Go-Round (Dizzy Izzy)

The first player in line runs to a baseball bat approximately 30 to 50 feet in front of the line, stands the bat up straight, places her palms down on top and her head on the back of her hands. Then the player walks around the bat eight times, drops it and runs back to the foot of the line. The second player repeats the run to the bat, picks up the bat as soon as it is dropped, and repeats the action of the first player. This game can be played as a relay race.

Mexican Cockfight

Equipment: Colored ribbon or strips of paper.
Method: Circle formation with leader standing in the center. The leader selects
   two players from the circle. They represent the two cocks. They stand back
   to back while the leader pins a piece of colored ribbon or paper on the back
   of each. The cocks then face each other. Each tries by moving or jumping
   about to discover the color of ribbon or paper on the back of his opponent,
   without letting the opponent catch a glimpse of the color on his own back.
   The winning cock is the one who first discovers the color of the ribbon or
   paper. These two cocks then return to the circle and two others are chosen.

Animal Chase

Two pens are marked off in distant corners of the play area. One player, the chaser, stands at one side of one of these pens. The other players stand within this pen. All of the players in the pen are named for different animals, there being several players of each kind. Thus, there may be a considerable number each of bears, deer, and foxes. The chaser calls the name of any animal he chooses as a signal for the players to run. For instance, he may call, "Bears," whereupon all of the players who represent bears must run across to the other pen, the chaser trying to catch them. Any player caught before reaching the opposite pen changes places with the chaser.

Bombardment

The play area is divided into two equal parts by a line marked across the center; boundary lines are marked along the sides, and goal lines across both ends. One team is placed in each court and an equal number of Indian clubs is placed across the width of the courts of each goal line. The players attempt to knock over the opponent's clubs with a ball thrown by a player from within his team's court. Each club that is knocked over scores one point. The club is scored and immediately set up again. Play is continuous until five points are made by either team. The team that first scores five points wins the game.

Two playground balls, basketballs, or volleyballs are used for the game. The game is started with a throw by a player from both teams made from his representative goal line. The ball may be thrown to a teammate or into the opponent's court at the start of the game and during the game. Balls must be thrown from where they are caught; however, balls that go out of bounds, including those which have knocked over a club, are recovered by a nearby player, brought into the court, and put into play at the point where the ball went out. Players cannot enter their opponent's court. If a player in any manner knocks over a club on his team's goal line, one point is awarded to his opponents.

Additional Comments:
- The leader should place scorekeepers in line with both goals to facilitate accurate scoring.

Variations:
- The teams may play until all of the clubs on either goal line are knocked down. The team wins which first knocks down all of the clubs on the opponent's goal line.

Keep Away

Two teams, each with six to eight players, are scattered over the play area. A ball is tossed into the area. The players attempt to recover the ball and pass it among their own team members while the opponents attempt to intercept the passes. If two opponents catch a pass simultaneously, the leader steps in to toss the ball between these two players, who try to bat the ball to their own team members. They cannot catch the ball on the tossup. This game is very informal. It is continuous and no points are scored.

Rules are often contributed by the players and boundaries, methods of handling the ball, and scores according to the number of successful passes illustrate factors which may be considered in making additional rules for Keep Away and converting it into a more complex game.

Additional Comments:
- The leader should encourage quick passing and accurate catching.
- The leader may use types of dress or uniforms, colored arm bands, or other familiar team divisions to identify the teams. The identity of the membership should be distinguished readily.
- The leader and the players should agree, before starting the game, upon a signal such as a whistle to stop the game. The players become very noisy and often it is difficult to get their attention.

Variations:
- A player may claim the ball if he tags an opponent while the opponent has the ball in his hands.

Last Couple out

The players are in couples in a double file formation. The player who is IT stands three to five feet in front of the first couple in the file, with his back toward the other players. He calls, "Last couple out!" Then, the two players of the last couple in the file separate and run forward on the outside of the file and attempt to catch hands in front of the one who is IT before either is tagged by IT. IT cannot turn to watch the two who are coming. If he tags one of the two players before they catch hands, the one whom he tags becomes his partner and the other player is IT. If he does not tag one of them, he is IT again. The couple takes its place at the head of the file and a new couple is the "last couple."

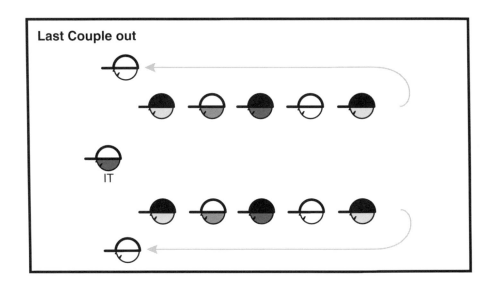

Last Couple out

Additional Comments:
- The leader should allow a space 60 feet ahead of the players in order that there will be plenty of room to run forward.
- The leader should instruct the players to move back one long step each time a couple takes its place at the head of the double file.
- The leader may change the game by having the one tagged become IT and his partner becomes the partner of the one who tagged him.
- The leader should use a small number of couples (about six). Organizing players into small groups permits more activity for each player.

Protect the King

One player, the king, sits on a stool in the center of a circle approximately 15 feet in diameter marked on the ground or floor. Another player is the guard and he stays inside the circle to protect the king. The other players are on the outside of the circle. They attempt to crown, or hit, the king below the waist with a playground ball. When a player crowns the king, he becomes the guard and the former guard becomes the king. The former king joins the group outside the circle.

Additional Comments:
- The leader should teach the guard to keep himself between the ball and the king and to block the ball with his feet or legs, but not to kick the ball. He may catch the ball to intercept it and return it to the players outside the circle.
- The leader may make the circle either smaller or larger depending on the skill level of the players.
- The leader should enforce the "no burn" rule (hard throwing up close) and throwing underhand.

Variations:
- The players may use two or three balls, allow the king to dodge the ball (the stool is removed), and allow the king to have two guards.

Protect the Pin

Same as Protect the King except a plastic bowling pin is used instead of the king. The pin is placed in the middle of another circle about three feet in diameter and the guards may not enter this circle.

Additional Comments:
- The leader should encourage the players to pass the balls to others if they do not have a clear shot at the pin. Fast movement and passing will make it more difficult for the guards to protect the pin.
- If a player has been the guard more than once, the leader may facilitate sportsmanship by encouraging the player to give up his spot as a guard to another player who has not had the opportunity. The game is more fun for all if everyone has at least one opportunity to be a guard.

Human Hurdle

Players form several teams with about eight players on each team. Each team sits in a circle on the floor with all players on the team facing the center of the circle; knees are straight, feet are together, and heels are kept on the floor. The several teams, or circles, are scattered over the play space.

One player in each team is designated as the starter. On a signal, the starter from each team jumps up, hurdles over the legs of each player in turn, and, as he reaches his place in the circle and takes his position on the floor, he tags the second runner. The second runner repeats the procedure and tags the third runner. Each player runs to the right and tags the player on his right. The team wins which first finishes with its last runner in his own place on the floor.

Wave Jump

Players stand in a circle facing the center. One player, holding a rope about 20-feet long, kneels in the center of the circle. A knotted towel is tied on the free end of the rope in order to weight that end. The center player turns the rope, playing it out to its full length until sufficient momentum keeps the weighted end of the rope turning under the feet of the players in the circle, who must jump over it. Any player who touches the rope with his feet while it is turning is out, and he leaves the circle. A player cannot step back from the circle to avoid touching the rope. The player who remains in the circle after the others have been put out turns the rope for the repetition of the game.

Line Tag

This is a tag game with the players scattered over the play area. The game starts with one player, IT, attempting to tag another player. The first player whom he tags joins hands with him and helps in tagging another player. Both may use only their free hands. Each player who is tagged joins hands with the one tagging him. The line grows longer as more players are tagged, and only the players at the two ends of the line can tag. They can tag only with their free hands. No tagging is considered a fair tag if the line has broken a hold at any place while the player is tagged. The game continues until all players have been tagged.

Additional Comments:
- The leader should limit the play area for a small group of players.
- The children may play with and without permitting the players to run under the arms of the line of taggers in order to avoid being tagged. Prohibiting this probably means that the line will have to corner a player in order to tag him.

Kickball

Everyone knows how to play kickball; however, there are several variations to this game.

Variation 1:
Kickball is played with a playground ball and on a softball diamond and can be played outdoors or indoors. Players form two equal teams with about 10 players on each team. The players on each team are numbered. The game is played with one player up to "bat" and one player from the other team in the field. For example, Player One from Team A stands behind the ball placed on home plate while Player One from Team B is in the field. Player One from Team A, the "batter," kicks the ball into the field, and runs and touches as many bases as he can before the fielder recovers the ball and runs to home base with it. The kicked ball is a foul ball if it hits the ground outside of the baselines from home plate to first and to third; the batter cannot run on a foul ball and must kick again. One point is given for each base touched by the batter, but he is out if he does not get to home before the fielder reaches it with the ball. The players on Team A kick in numerical order, and the players on the opposing team with the same number as the batter field the ball, until three outs are called. Then, Team B kicks in numerical order with the players on Team B playing in the field.

The game is played for a designated length of time and the team that scored the most points in the period wins the game. Or a definite number of innings are played, with each team up to bat three, five, or seven times, and the team that scores the most points at the end of the designated number of innings is the winner.

Additional Comments:
- The leader should acquaint the players, in this simple game, with the softball diamond and softball terms such as *out* and *foul.*
- The leader may allow the players to run at the ball before kicking it.

- The leader may enlarge the home base by enclosing the home plate within a long base (about three-by-six-feet); this minimizes the hazard of collisions as the two runners are coming in to the home base.

Variation 2:
This kickball variation is somewhat similar to Variation 1, except, when the kicker kicks the ball (anywhere in the play area—there are no foul balls), whoever fields the ball stands in place where he fields the ball and all other team members rush to line up behind the person fielding the ball. Once lined up, they pass the ball over their heads (or between their legs). If the kicker who is running around the bases at the same time reaches home plate before the last fielder has possession of the ball, a run is scored.

Likewise, if the fielders complete the overhead passing before the runner reaches home plate an out is called. Each person on the team has the opportunity to kick once. Outs are not tallied, only runs scored. Because of the "no foul ball" rule, this game is best played indoors.

Variation 3:
Again, this variation is similar to Variation 2, except this time when the ball is kicked, whoever fields the ball throws the ball back to the pitcher or designated fielder. The pitcher then either with that ball, or using a basketball which may be placed next to the pitcher must run with the ball and make a basket before the runner reaches home plate. Obviously this is played indoors in a gym with a basketball hoop. The leader should make sure there is a new pitcher each "inning," or perhaps a new pitcher for each new kicker to give everyone an opportunity to sink a basket.

Team Ball

A large ball such as an earthball or beachball is used. The players form two teams with from 10 to 12 players on each team. Each team is scattered over one of the two courts separated by a net or rope from six- to eight-feet high. Side and end boundaries enclose the courts. Play is started by a player on one team, chosen by chance. The players throw the ball back and forth over the net attempting to hit the floor of the opponents' court with the ball. A point is made if the ball thrown over the net hits the floor of the opponents' court. No point is made if the ball is caught by the opponents before it hits the floor. Play is continuous; after a point is made, the ball is recovered and put into play immediately. Any ball going outside the boundary lines is recovered by the nearest player, who brings it into the court at the point where it went out and puts it into play. The team that makes the most points wins the game.

Additional Comments:
- The leader should appoint a scorekeeper or teach the children to referee the game as he keeps score.
- The leader should teach the players to pass the ball among their team members to obtain an advantage in scoring. The leader should stress the importance of each team's covering the court and of players' playing their places on the court. He should also discourage holding the ball.
- The leader may add features from volleyball and make additional rules according to the skill of the players, for example, acquaint players with rotation, scoring, setup, and serving.

Variations:
- The game may be played with two balls rather than only one.

First Base Ball

This game uses a softball, a junior softball bat, a pitcher's box, home plate, and first base. The game is played by four or more players and it is popular whenever there are not enough players for other types of softball games. The four necessary players are the pitcher, catcher, batter, and fielder. If there are more players, they are fielders, who are numbered first, second, and so on, depending upon the number of players. The players adopt such softball rules as are desirable for the particular group. Each player scores for himself alone when he is the batter.

The batter scores by hitting a fair ball and running to first base and back to home plate without being put out. The batter may be put out by another player catching a fly or foul ball, by the catcher tagging home plate with the ball before the runner touches the plate, or by three strikes.

When the batter is put out, the players rotate position. The batter becomes the fielder (or the last fielder if there are more than four players), the fielder (or the first fielder) becomes the pitcher, the pitcher becomes the catcher, and the catcher becomes the batter.

Additional Comments:
- The leader should use this game only with very small groups of players. However, he may teach children how to play the game for home and neighborhood play.

500

As in First Base Ball, this game is usually played with a smaller number of players. It can be played with either a kickball, softball, or Wiffle ball, and indoors or outdoors. In this game, there is the batter (or kicker, depending on the size of the ball), a pitcher and the rest are fielders. As the batter hits the ball, the fielders attempt to field the ball. If a person in the field catches the ball on the fly, he scores 250 points; if he fields the ball on one hop, he scores 100 points; if he fields the ball as the ball is rolling (or more than one bounce), he scores 50 points. The game continues until a fielder has accumulated 500 points (or any other predetermined total). He then becomes the pitcher, the pitcher becomes the batter (kicker), and the game continues. When a new game begins, all fielders begin with zero points.

Overtake

The players stand in a circle and count off by twos. Those numbered one are members of one team and those numbered two are members of the other team. Each team selects a captain, and the two captains stand inside of a six-foot circle in the center of the circle of players which is now composed of two teams with no two players from the same team standing next to each other. Both captains have a ball. On the signal to start, each captain, starting with any team member in the circle whom he chooses, tosses it to the next team member (in a clockwise direction) who tosses it back to the captain. The ball is tossed in this manner clockwise around the circle by both teams at the same time until each ball has been thrown to all members of each team and is back in the captain's hands. One team *overtakes* the other team when its ball passes the ball of the other team as the balls are tossed around the circle. The team that tosses the ball completely around the circle as described and finishes with its ball in the hands of the captain, scores one point; when a team *overtakes* and finishes first, it scores two points. The team first scoring five points wins the game.

Additional Comments:
- The leader should explain and enforce response to the signal used to start the tosses and use the same signal for each start.
- The game may be played with various kinds of balls and different types of throws and passes.

Push Ball Relay

Teams are in a relay formation. Each player, in turn, pushes a basketball with a wand or stick over the goal line. The game is varied by:

1. pushing the ball over the goal line, picking it up, and carrying it back to the next player who waits behind the starting line;

2. carrying the ball to the goal line and pushing it back over the starting line; or
3. pushing it both to the goal line and back across the starting line.

The team wins which finishes first.

Additional Comments:
- Suggestions for teaching relays are included with the description of Simple Relay.

Circle Tag

Approximately 10 to 12 players stand in a circle formation equidistant from each other. Upon a signal, all run in a clockwise direction around the circle. Each player tries to tag the player in front of him, while at the same time, the player just in back of him is trying to tag him. When a player is tagged, he drops out of the game, turning toward the center of the circle where he awaits the finish of the game with other players who have been tagged. The last player left in the chase is the winner.

Additional Comments:
- The leader may use this game as a warm-up activity, and play only once or twice at any one time. The players should be three to four feet apart in the circle. The leader should watch the players remaining near the finish since the game can be very fatiguing for the last players. Often, the game must be stopped before a winner is declared.

Variations:
- A whistle may be used as a signal while the players are running; the players must turn and run in the opposite direction when the whistle is blown.
- This game may be played with a large number of players in one circle. The players are numbered from one to four. When the leader calls a number, only the players with that number run; those who are tagged go to the center and those who are not tagged, return to their places in the circle and run when their number is called again. Players attempt to be the last one with their number left in the circle.

Balloon Stomp

Each player has a balloon tied around her ankle. On a signal from the leader, the players try to burst each other's balloons by attempting to stomp on the balloon, at the same time trying to avoid having their balloons being burst. This is also a good warm-up activity, and should be played only once or twice.

File Relay

Teams are in a relay formation. Each player places his hands on the hips of the player just ahead of him. At the signal, the whole file runs to the goal and back. The game is varied by:

1. dividing large teams into small units of three or four players running in file formation and touching off the next unit in their team as they return from the goal line;
2. placing Indian clubs on the goal which the file must circle before returning; or
3. placing three Indian clubs about eight feet apart along the path to the goal for each team and requiring the players to weave around them as they progress to and from the goal.

The team wins which finishes the relay first.

Additional Comments:
- A foul is counted against the team if it "breaks" the file while running.
- The leader should teach the players to hold the player in front of them with their hands on the bony structure at the sides of the hips. They should not hold other players with their hands tugging against the softer structure of the abdomen.
- When using Indian clubs, the team is required to set up any club which it knocks down before continuing the race.

Run, Sheep, Run

The players form two teams. Each team chooses a player to be its captain. A goal area is designated, and one team stays at the goal while the other team hides. After the players are hidden, the captain of the hiding team comes back and accompanies the other team, whose object is to find the hiders and then reach the goal before the opponents do. The team that has all of its members back in the goal area first wins. Any member of the searching team who finds the hiders tells his captain, then the captain calls, "Run, sheep, run!" Upon this signal, all players must return to the goal. The captain of the hiders team may call, "Run, sheep, run!" as a signal at any time he feels that the searchers are far enough away for his team to reach the goal in safety. Both teams must run for the goals if either captain calls that signal. Each team, when hiding, plans signals which the captain uses in calling warnings to his team, for example, *red* may mean danger, *green* may mean get ready to run, *cucumber* may mean come in closer, and *tiger* may mean to go back.

Additional Comments:
* The players should be allowed to originate their own signals. These may be colors, birds, or vegetables. Each signal holds a meaning known only by one team.

Buddy Relay

The teams are in relay formation behind the starting line. One player of each team is standing on the goal line and facing his team. On the signal to start, this player runs to the first player in the team, grasps his hand, and runs with him back to the goal line. He remains there while the player whom he brought to the goal line goes back to the team and gets the next player until all have been rescued and are in file formation back of the goal line. The team that finishes first wins the relay.

Slip Away Tag

A large group of players are divided into units of five to six players. These units are scattered over the play area with the players in each unit sitting in a small circle. Each circle of players has a small object which is passed from hand to hand around the circle during the game. There are two extra players, one who is IT and another who is the runner. The runner carries an object identical to that held by the players in the circle. The player who is IT tries to tag the runner, who can save himself by stepping inside any circle; then the player in that circle who holds the object becomes the runner. He must get up and run. As soon as he gets up, IT gives chase and tries to tag him. The runner who steps into a circle to save himself sits down and becomes a part of the circle of players, and the object which he carried is started around the circle.

When the player who is IT tags a runner, the runner gives the object which he carried to him and the chaser becomes the runner while the player who was tagged becomes IT and the game is continued.

Additional Comments:
* Any small object such as a small eraser, a crumpled piece of paper, or a piece of ribbon may be used. The leader should avoid accidental tripping by requiring players to sit cross-legged and to keep their knees down.

Steal the Bacon

The players are divided into two equal teams of from eight to ten players. A small circle is drawn in the center of the play area and an Indian club or a knotted towel, the "bacon," is placed in this circle. A goal line is drawn across both ends of the play area and one team stands behind each goal line. The players in each team are numbered beginning with one and continuing through as many numbers as there are players on each team. The teams being equal in number of individuals, the numbers are duplicated in both teams. The leader calls a number. The two players having that number run and attempt to get the bacon. The one who is successful in carrying the bacon back to his goal without being tagged by the other player scores two points for his team. If he is tagged while he has the bacon and before he reaches the goal, the tagger scores one point for his team. If a player touches the bacon but fails to pick it up, his opponent can score one point by tagging him or picking it up and returning it to his goal without being tagged for two points.

The game continues as player's numbers are called by the leader. The team that scores 10 points first, or scores the most points within the allotted playing time, wins the game.

Additional Comments:
- The leader should teach the players that the chances for scoring are better if they do not grab the bacon at once and if they try to catch the other player off guard before picking up the bacon. He or she should teach them to keep in readiness to run in either direction and to pick up the bacon only when they can take off for their goal quickly. The leader may save time by requesting the player who has run toward his opponents' goal to bring back the bacon and place it in the center as he returns to his own goal.
- As in Line Soccer, more than one number may be called at a time to encourage teamwork.
- If more than one number at a time is called (e.g., numbers two and three), passing among teammates is allowed; however, if the pass falls incomplete and touches the ground, the opposite team scores one point—just as if they were tagged.

Sports Relay

Various sports techniques are used in relays. Some suggestions:

- *Soccer Dribble I:* A soccer ball is dribbled in a figure-eight pattern around two Indian clubs, to a goal, and back.
- *Soccer Dribble II:* A soccer ball is dribbled to a goal and back.

- *Softball Throw:* Each file has a catcher on a goal line approximately 35 feet from the starting line. Players run to a throwing line about 10 feet from the starting line, receive the ball from the catcher, throw it to the catcher, and tag off the next player waiting on the starting line, who runs to the throwing line, and so on.
- *Juggle:* Players juggle a ball over a rope, recover it, juggle it in back of and over the rope in the opposite direction; and then recover it and pass it to the next player waiting on the starting line.
- *Centering:* Players center a football down a file of players placed about seven feet apart. The last player in the file carries the ball to the starting line at the head of the file and starts the ball down the file again, and the relay continues until all are in their original positions. A center relay may be timed and the team wins which completes the passing of the ball from the first player to the last player on the team in the shortest period of time.
- *Basketball Pass:* Two players from each team progress to a goal and back as they pass and catch the ball. A player cannot progress while he has the ball in his hands.
- *Football Pass:* A football is passed as a Zigzag Relay; or the ball is passed from player to player down the lineup until a pass is missed. A team is out after from one to five misses and the team that stays in the longest wins the game.

Additional Comments:
- Other types of techniques or sports may be adapted to the relay pattern of play.

Line Basketball

Two teams line up in file formation at the free throw line on a basketball court. A player from Team One steps up to the free throw line and attempts to make a free throw. If he does make a free throw, then a player from Team Two steps up to the free throw line. If this player misses the free throw, he is out of the game. If he makes the free throw, then the next member of Team One must make the shot or is out of the game. This keeps going back and forth until someone misses and is out of the game. If the player from Team One makes the free throw, the player from Team Two must make the free throw or he is out of the game. If the player from Team One does not make the free throw, the player from Team Two does not need to make the free throw to stay in the game. After a player makes a free throw, or if he missed his free throw (and the previous player from the other team missed), he goes to the end of his team line and the next in line shoots next. The game continues, each team alternating until one team eliminates all the players from the opposing team.

Additional Comments:
  • If the free throw line is too far away for most players, the leader should move the teams closer to the basket until most players have a reasonable chance for success.

Three Steps

Three steps is played with a junior football. The playing field, 60 or more feet long, is marked with side boundary lines and goal lines. From two to ten players form each of two teams (Team A and Team B). The ball is passed by each team in turn and whenever the ball is passed over the opponent's line, a point is scored.

The two teams are on opposite ends of the field defending their own goal lines. The game is started by a player from either selected by chance. Upon the signal from the referee, the selected player (Team A) passes the ball from his own goal line toward Team B's goal. Either the ball is thrown over Team B's players and their goal line and scores a point, or the players from Team B attempt to catch the pass. If the pass is caught by Team B, the catcher takes three steps toward Team A's goal, and he passes from that spot attempting to score by throwing the ball over Team A's goal line. However, if the pass is not caught by the receiving team, it must be passed by the player who first touched

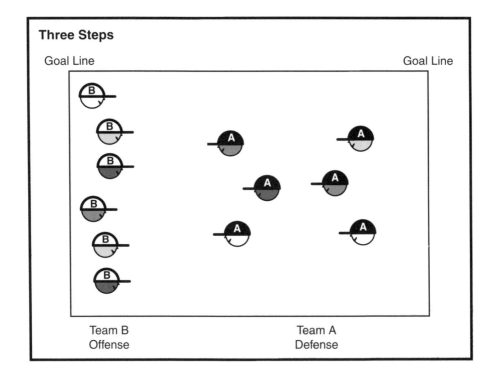

it. The defending team may attempt to prevent the ball from passing over its goal line by intercepting or batting down the ball.

When a ball goes over a side boundary line before it is touched by a player on the receiving team, it is recovered by a nearby player on the receiving team and played from a spot three steps inside the boundary line at the point where the ball went out of bounds.

Play is continuous with each team passing (offense) and receiving (defense) alternately until one team scores, or succeeds in passing the ball over the opponents' goal line. After a score is made, the ball is put into play by the team scored against from its goal line. The length of the playing period is determined by the players before the game is started. The team that scores the most points within the playing time, wins the game.

Additional Comments:
- The leader may limit play to passing or to punting, or he or she may permit both passing and punting.
- The leader may permit players to adopt football rules and scoring to their game or to originate suitable rules, but should not permit elementary school players to block, tackle, trip, or perform any other play which involves body contact.
- The number of permitted steps may be changed if the game is slow. Children often play the game as five steps or six steps.

Streets and Alleys

The players are arranged in equal lines containing an equal number of players. When the players face the front of the room and join hands, the aisles which form between the lines are called streets, and when they face the side of the room and join hands the aisles are called alleys. There are two extra players: one who is IT and one who is the runner. The player who is IT chases the runner who can run only through the aisles formed by the players. These aisles are changed when the leader calls, "Streets," or "Alleys." When *street* is called, all quickly face the front and join hands; and when *alley* is called, all quickly face the side and join hands again. Changing the aisles may either assist or hinder IT in tagging the runner. When the runner is tagged a new runner and chaser are selected and the original two players take their places in the lines of the participants.

Additional Comments:
- The leader may vary the time between changes so that his streets and alleys signals come unexpectedly. At times, the leader may help the runner, and at other times hinder the runner in calling the signals.

- If the tagger is slow in tagging, the leader may change the players so that the tagger becomes the runner and the runner becomes the tagger; or the leader may select two new players.
- The leaders may describe directions according to the situation. Perhaps "north" and "east" will be more suitable than "front" and "side."

Stealing Sticks (Capture the Flag)

Stealing Sticks is played like Prisoner's Base except that the element of stealing booty from the opponents is added to the game. Three or four sticks are kept in areas about three- or four-feet square, back of the left-hand end of each team's goal line, or on the opposite end of the team's prison. The teams try to capture the opponents as prisoners and to take their sticks without being tagged. The game is played until one team has all the sticks and has no one in prison.

Only one stick can be taken at a time. A player may return safely to his base upon tagging an opponent, freeing a prisoner, or stealing a stick.

Variations:
- A flag may be planted behind one end of each team's goal line. The opponents attempt to capture the flag in the same manner used in stealing the sticks. The game may end when the flag is captured and all teammates are out of prison.

Zigzag Relay

The players form two equal teams with 10 to 12 players on each team. The players in each team are arranged in two lines facing each other and several feet apart. They are placed so that those in one line stand opposite the spaces between the players in the line which they are facing. A ball is passed zigzag from the first player in one line to the first player in the other line and so on in zigzag pattern to the end. The first throw is started on a signal, and the team that finishes first wins the relay.

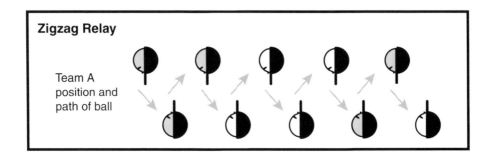

Zigzag Relay

Team A
position and
path of ball

Additional Comments:
- Different types of balls may be used, or the types of throws may be varied, such as underhand, overhand, and chest. The passes continue from the end back through the zigzag path to the player who started the ball.

Hip Tag

The player who is IT has a rolled newspaper or knotted towel with which he tags the other players. Those whom he tags assist him by holding other players and calling, "Hip!" They hold the players for him until he can tag them. Each player attempts to be the last one tagged.

Additional Comments:
- The leader should caution players against hitting too hard in tagging. They need only to touch the player whom they are tagging.

Indian Club Relay

Several teams are arranged in files behind a starting line. A circle is drawn on the floor in front of each file. In a straight line in front of each file, three Xs are marked on the floor six feet apart, with the first X marked six feet in front of the circle. An Indian club is placed on each X. The players run as for a relay, tagging off each team member in turn.

The first player in each file, starting on signal, brings the three clubs, one at a time, and places them inside the circle in front of his team. The second player takes the clubs from the circle one at a time and places them back on the three Xs. The third player brings the clubs back to the circle, and so on. The clubs must remain standing after each change. If a club falls, the player must return and set up the club before picking up the next club or tagging the next runner. The team that first finishes with all of its players back in their original places wins.

Additional Comments:
- The leader should guard against overfatigue. The game is strenuous and exciting. The game may be made more exciting by requiring the runner to handle the club with only one hand and to hold the other hand behind his back. Potatoes may be substituted for the Indian clubs for an old-fashioned potato race.

Concealed Words

The object is to discover the words concealed in sentences. The leader will give each player a paper and a pencil and dictate a proverb. Each player will work independently and write all the words he can find in the sentence. All words must be made up of letters used in the exact order in which they appear in the sentence. No one-letter words are allowed. For example, in the proverb "Barking dogs don't bite," the concealed words are *bark, ark, kin, king, in, do, dog, don, on, bit,* and *it.*

Kaleidoscope

Four to eight players stand in a row across the front of the room, and are named certain colors. The others close their eyes while the colors change places. Anyone who can name the colors and put them back in their first positions may do so. The names of flowers, birds, or trees may be substituted for colors.

Blind Walk

The starting line is six-feet long. A ball is placed as the goal, 90 feet in front of the starting line. All but one player stands behind the starting line. The extra player stands by the goal and has a whistle.

The first player behind the starting line is blindfolded. The blindfolded player spins about three times on the starting line and then stands still. The player at the goal blows the whistle. The blindfolded player faces the sound of the whistle and takes 30 steps in that direction. Here, he removes his blindfold

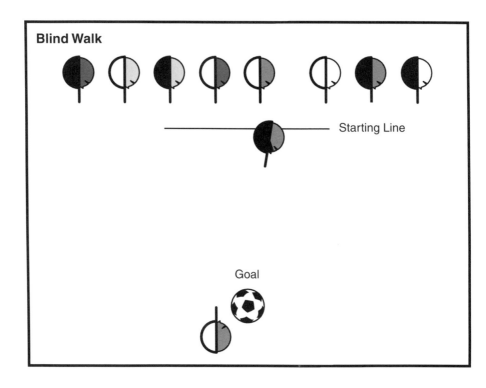

Blind Walk

Starting Line

Goal

and the point of his heel for the thirtieth step is marked. The remaining players each in turn make the walk. While one player is walking forward, the next should be adjusting his blindfold. The player whose mark is nearest the goal wins. Players at the line should not give directions to walking contestants.

My Cat

This game puts the players in a circle and each in turn describes "my cat" with a word beginning with the letter *A*. For instance, the first player may say, "My cat is an awful cat," the second, "My cat is an ambitious cat," and so on. The same adjective may be used only *once*. When a player cannot think of a word in a moment or so, the leader counts to five slowly and if the player has not called an adjective, he fails. Players who fail twice must pay a forfeit after the contest is over.

Horse and Rider

The players take partners with one player in each couple on the back of his partner. The horse is in an upright position and not on all fours. The object for each rider is to pull any one of the other riders off of his horse. The game starts when all are ready. A rider who is dismounted becomes his partner's horse. The rider who meets all comers and remains seated on his horse wins.

Round the Bases

The players are divided into two teams. One team lines up at second base, the other lines up at home plate. If there are enough teams, they may line up behind all bases. On a signal to start, the first player for each team starts around the four bases, touching off the second player at the base he started from. The team finishing first wins.

Running over three feet outside the baseline and failure to touch each base are fouls.

Racing the Ball

The players are divided into two equal teams. One team is in a circle formation and the other is in a row with the first player in the row about three feet away from the circle. Players in the circle face inside, and the players in the row face the circle. The player in the circle standing closest to the row is given a ball. At a signal, the ball is bounce passed to the right from player to player around the circle. It must be bounce passed completely around the circle as many times as there are players on the opponents' team. At the same time the first player in the row runs around the circle. When the first player finishes, the second player begins to run around the circle. This race continues until all members of this team run around the circle. The team finishing first wins. When players fumble the ball, they must retrieve it and return to position before bounce passing it on. The two teams reverse after each turn.

Circle Relay

The players are divided into several teams of equal number and arranged in single file facing a common center, so that the lines radiate from the center like spokes of a wheel (see illustration). The last person on each team faces around to the right and at a signal from the leader runs around the outside of the circle faster than the runners of the opposing teams, returns to her team, and touches the outstretched hand of the next runner in line. This person then runs her turn.

Additional Comments:
- A player may start only after she is touched by the incoming player on her team.
- A runner may pass any one of her opposing runners.
- As soon as the incoming player has touched off the next runner in line, she takes a place at the head of the line in the center of the circle.

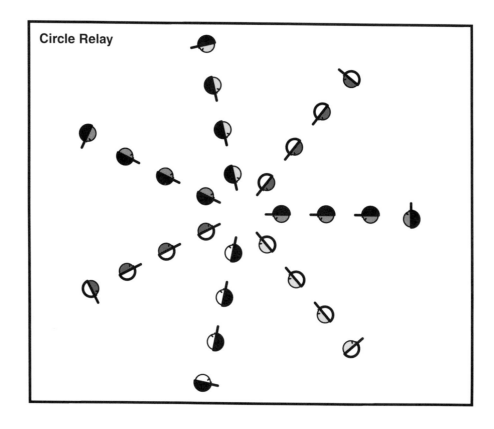

Circle Relay

Poisoned Book

The players hold hands or wrists in a circle around a book that is standing up in the middle of the circle. The players then pull each other forward and backward trying to force one player to knock the book over. If a player steps on or knocks the book over, he is eliminated. This can continue until there is a winner.

Variations:
- If an Indian club is used, the game may be called Poisoned Stake.
- The group may form more than one circle with a book within the circle. When enough players are eliminated, a new circle is formed or else the winning persons from each of the circles form a circle and determine the winner.

Grizzly Bear

This game is usually played with boys' caps, but knotted handkerchiefs or balls of crumpled paper may be used. One player is the grizzly bear; he is blindfolded and stands in a stride position with his feet wide apart sideways. The other players stand in turn at a point five to ten feet behind him, and throw their caps forward as far as possible between his legs. After the caps are all thrown, each player moves forward and stands beside his own cap. The bear walks on all fours, still blindfolded, until he reaches a cap. The player whose cap is first touched at once becomes an object of chase by the other players, who are at liberty to pommel him (with their caps) when he is captured. He then becomes the grizzly bear for the next round.

Boston

Players are seated in a circle on benches or chairs. There is one fewer chairs than participants. One participant without a chair stands in the circle. The center player calls out periodically, "Change right," whereupon everyone who is seated must change places, moving only in the designated direction, while he rushes for an empty chair. If he should capture it, the person who failed to fill it in time must go into the center. The game thus continues indefinitely.

Additional Comments:
- This game can be used equally well for grown people in community gatherings and affords much amusement.
- The person in the center may call any direction, such as left, diagonal, and across.

Marbles

Equipment: Plan of game and playing regulations.
Generic marbles: Two to four players; 12 marbles plus one shooter for each player.
Method: A circle eight feet in diameter is drawn. Twelve or more marbles are placed in the center of the circle. Players lag to determine the order of play. When shooting, players must hold their shooting hand on the ground at the rim of the circle. All shots must be made without moving hands. The first player shoots at the marbles in the center of the ring and tries to knock them outside the circle. When a marble is knocked completely out of the circle, a point is scored. A player continues to shoot as long as he knocks a marble out of the circle. When a player knocks a marble out and his shooter stays in the circle, he shoots from where the shooter stopped. If a player fails to knock the marble out of the circle, he loses his turn and the next player shoots.

Cincy

A circle four feet in diameter is drawn. A starting line is drawn 10 to 15 feet away from the circle. A line parallel to the starting line is drawn across the center of the circle. Players decide the number of marbles to be used. Marbles are placed on the center line. Players lag to determine the order of shooting. Players shoot from the starting line. The second shot is taken from where the shooter stops on the first turn. When a marble is knocked completely out of the circle, a point is scored. If a player hits another player's shooter, the player is out of the game and must return all marbles he has knocked out of the circle to the middle line. When all marbles on the center line have been knocked out of the circle, the player having the most points is the winner.

Dead Line

A small circle 14 inches in diameter is drawn. Five to ten marbles are placed in the center of the circle. A dead line is drawn three feet from the circle. A shooting line is drawn 10 feet from the dead line. Players lag to determine the order of shooting. A player is out of the game if his first shot stops between the starting line and the dead line or if his shooter stops in the circle. Otherwise the game is like Cincy.

Chasers

Players should decide on playing limits. Each player uses one marble. Players lag to determine the order of shooting. The first player shoots his marble, and the others follow in turn. The object of the game is for players to keep their marbles out of one another's way in order not to be killed but to keep them in a position to hit another player's marble. When a player hits another player's marble, the player hit is killed and goes out of the game. A player hitting another player's marble takes a second shot. The game continues until all players have been killed except one. This player is the winner.

Picking Plum

Two parallel lines are drawn four to eight feet apart. Either line may be the plum line and the other the shooting line. Each player places two or more marbles on the plum line, one to two inches apart. Players lag to determine the order of shooting. Players shoot from the shooting line, keeping a hand on the ground to shoot. When a player knocks a marble off the plum line, he scores one point. Players take one shot in order. If a player fails to knock a marble off the plum line, he must place another marble on the line. When all the marbles have been knocked off the plum line, players add up points, or the number of marbles they have knocked off the plum line. The one with the most points is the winner.

Corner Spy

The group is divided into four teams and each team stands in a separate corner of the room. A circle 10 feet in diameter is drawn in the center of the room. Each team chooses a captain and the captains take a position in the circle in the center of the room. Each captain has a beanbag. At a signal, each captain starts tossing the beanbag to each member of his team. As each player receives it, he tosses it back and squats. As the captain tosses to the last player in his group, he yells, "Corner spy," and runs for the head of his team. The last player upon receiving the bag runs for the center of the room and immediately repeats the performance of the first captain. All of the players rise to stand on the signal, "Corner spy." This continues until all have acted as captain. The team finishing with its first captain in position in the center first wins.

Purgatory

Four holes (three or four inches in diameter) are made in a square formation. The holes should be 8 to 10 feet apart. A fifth hole is made in the center of the square (purgatory). A starting line is drawn four feet from the first hole. Players lag to determine the order of shooting. The first player shoots from the starting line toward Hole 1. If this players shoots his marble into Hole 1, he shoots from the rim of Hole 1 toward Hole 2. If he fails to shoot his marble into Hole 1, the next player shoots. When a player hits another player's marble, he gets another shot. Players shoot for Hole 1, Hole 2, Hole 3, Hole 4, and then into the center hole (purgatory). From the center hole, players shoot to Hole 1. On his next turn, a player who successfully returned his marble to Hole 1 moves a hand's span from the rim of each hole and shoots for the next hole. After each successful return to Hole 1, another span is added. Players should decide the number of spans for the game. The usual number is four or five. When a player shooting from the center hole to Hole 1 hits another player's marble, the player hit puts his marble into the center hole and he must start the game over again. When a player has successfully completed the number of spans for the game, he becomes a killer. Any player whose marble is hit by a killer is out of the game.

Gorilla Hunt

This game requires a long rope and two paper swatters. Two players are blindfolded. The leader places the rope in an irregular trail on the ground. The players crawl along the trail following the rope, find the swatters, and encounter the opponent. The first player hit on the head is eliminated from the game and the winner takes on another opponent in the new game.

Chinese Puzzle Game

One player is IT. He turns his back to the group. The other players form a chain by clasping hands with the player in front and behind. The leader then leads the chain in and out over and under the hands into any position possible without dropping hands. IT is called to untangle the chain without breaking the links.

Balloon Goal

The game is played with two balloons, preferably 12 inches in diameter, one red and one blue, which are struck with the open hand only. If the air of the balloon is exhausted, the balloon may be refilled with breath, whereupon the

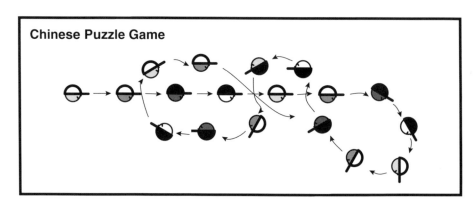

Chinese Puzzle Game

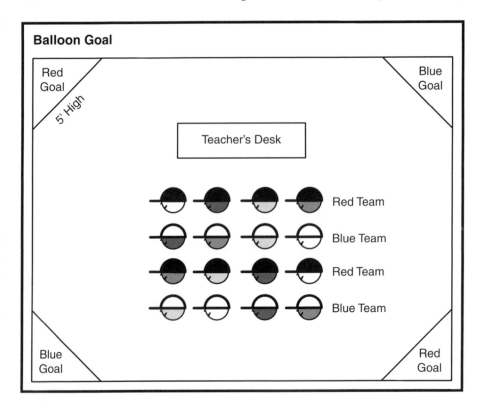

balloon will be found to still float sufficiently in the air for the purposes of the game.

The class is divided into two teams, preferably designated by colors corresponding to the balloons, worn on the arm or otherwise. The teams are assigned by rows across the room from side to side, the first row of players belonging to the red team, the second to the blue, the third to the red. Four goals are formed by stretching a tape diagonally across each of the four corners of the room about five feet from the floor, the goals in the diagonally opposite corners having the same colors, two of red and two of blue (see illustration). The game consists of hitting the balloon with the open hand so that it will float down behind a goal tape, the red balloon scoring when it enters the red goals and the blue balloon scoring when it enters the blue goals. There are no real guards, but it is the object of all players belonging to the red team to get the red balloon into the red goals, and of the blue team to keep it out. Similarly, the object of the blue team is to get the blue balloon into the blue goals and of the red team to keep it out.

The game starts by the leader putting the balloons in play by tossing them up in the center of the room, and then each side immediately begins to play for them. A scorekeeper notes one point for each team making a goal with its balloon, but the game continues without interruption, the balloon being at once put into play again by the leader. A game can last however long the leader and the players desire; however, two shorter games of 10 minutes may be preferable to one game of 20 minutes.

Outside Tag Ball

All but two of the players are arranged in a circle, with the players standing at four foot intervals facing in. The two players not a part of the circle are IT and stand outside of and at opposite sides of the circle. At a signal, the players of the circle pass a ball about. The two ITs endeavor to touch the ball by running about the outside of the circle. Either IT touching the ball exchanges places with the player responsible for his touching it. If the ball falls to the floor, the player responsible must recover it. If he has to break his position in the circle to do this, however, one of the ITs may step in to the place if he can. If an IT gets a place in this way, the absent player becomes IT. The players who are IT are not allowed to enter the circle, but must confine their activities to the outside.

Army Ball

All but one of the players is in a large U with the players four feet apart and facing in. Each player marks his position by placing the initials of his rank on the floor. Starting at the right end of the U the players are named general, colonel, major, captain, lieutenant, sergeant and corporal, the balance of the players being privates (see illustration). At the signal to start, the players pass a playground ball about. Any player responsible for the ball striking the floor must recover it. As soon as the ball strikes the floor, the players scatter. When the player who dropped the ball recovers it, he attempts to hit one of the players. The U then re-forms and the player who dropped the ball, as well as any player hit by him, fall in at the left of the U, and the other players move to the right to take the positions vacated. To score a fair hit, the ball must hit the

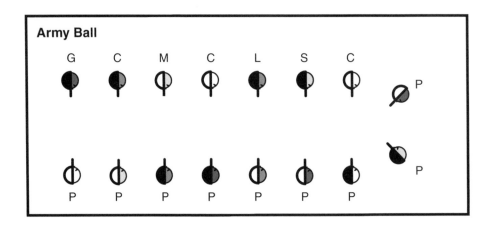

player on the fly. Once it has hit the floor it is dead. At a signal, the ball is put in play again, and the game continues. The object of the game obviously is to secure and hold the highest rank possible.

Hook Arm Tag

All but two of the players are arranged in a single circle facing in. The players are in pairs with a five-foot interval between each pair. Each pair of players links inside arms, and places the outside hand on the hip. The two players who are not a part of the circle are on opposite sides of the circle, and one of them is IT, the other one is the runner. At a signal, IT chases the runner with the object of tagging him. The runner runs about the circle as he wishes and finally hooks on to the extended elbow of one of the players in the circle. The player whose arm is hooked stands fast; the other player now becomes the runner, and IT takes after him. If IT tags the runner, the two reverse places and the game continues.

The Ocean Is Stormy

All but two players are in pairs scattered about the playing area. Each pair draws a circle three feet in diameter about its position. Each pair joins hands and secretly chooses the name of some fish. The extra players are whales and start in the center of the playing area holding hands. At a signal, the whales, continuing to hold hands, walk about the playing area calling the names of fish. Each pair that has the name of the fish that they have accepted, called, falls in behind the whales and follows after them. When the whales can think of no more fish, they call, "The ocean is stormy," and all run for the empty circles. The pair left without a circle becomes the whales for the next game.

Grocery Store

The first player begins by saying, "I went to the grocery store and bought some _____." The second player repeats the statement and adds another commodity to it. Each succeeding player repeats all that has been said and adds one purchase to the list. When a player fails to repeat the list in order, he drops out, and the next player attempts it.

Variations:
- This can be varied by "packing a suitcase and putting in _____" or "going on a hike and visiting _____."

Gossip

The players are in a circle or square. The leader begins the game by whispering a statement very rapidly in the ear of the person sitting next to him. The statements or assumed words are passed on by the same method from person to person until the last person. He is to tell what he thought was whispered in his ear. Then the leader tells what he actually told the first person.

Alphabet Cards

This is played with two teams. Each person has a letter of the alphabet painted on a card. The leader calls out a word to Team A. If the members of Team A spell the word correctly in one minute, they score a point for their team and are given another word to spell. If they fail to spell the word correctly or take more than one minute, then Team B gets a chance. The leader should list the words in advance (to make sure that each letter is in possession of one of the players). Play should progress from easy to hard.

Double Circle Ball

All but one of the players is arranged in a double circle—the players in the rear covering the players of the front circle at normal distances, pairs standing four feet apart. The extra player is IT and is outside of the circle. At a signal, the players of the inner circle pass a ball about. Each player upon receiving the ball passes it to another player and immediately changes positions with the player behind. IT runs about the circle, attempting to secure either of these player's positions before the change is completed. Any players responsible for the ball touching the floor or any player losing his place to IT, becomes IT. The two change places and the game continues.

Hunter, Fox, and Gun

Two lines of players stand on opposite sides of the room facing each other. The head player of each line decides whether the line shall represent hunters, foxes, or guns. Then each runs down his line, whispering this information to the players. The leaders stay at the foot of the lines so that for the next game each line will have a new head. When the leader counts one, two, three each line walks three steps, falls into position, and makes the noise of the object it is representing. Hunters stand with hands on hips and say, "Oh." Guns pretend to shoot a gun and say, "Bang." Foxes must put their thumbs in their ears, wave their fingers at the other line and cry, "Yip, yip, yip." Points are scored on the following basis: foxes defeat hunters, hunters defeat guns, and guns defeat foxes. If both teams represent the same thing, neither one scores.

Poison Areas

Four to eight circles three feet in diameter are established in scattered positions along the edges of the playing area—these are poisoned areas. The players are arranged in a single column of files from four to ten feet apart about the outside of the playing area. The players should be in a more or less circular formation passing through the poisoned area. The leader starts playing music at the same time the group starts walking around the playing area in time to the music, marching through the circles. All of a sudden the music is stopped. The group stops marching at the same time. People who are standing so that either foot touches a poisoned area is eliminated and sit on the floor in the center of the playing area. The players may not leap over the poisoned areas, but must walk through them at the normal cadence and stop instantly with the music. After those who have been eliminated are seated, the music is started and the group marches around as before. This continues until all but one player have been eliminated. This player is the winner.

Muffin Pan Penny Toss

An ordinary muffin pan is needed. Cardboard disks are cut out so that they fit into the bottom of each compartment of the muffin pan. A book is set on end against the wall and the pan leans against it with the top edge at an angle. A throwing line is drawn nine feet away from the pan. Each player is given three pennies or better still, washers the size of pennies. The players throw in turn, each tossing three pennies each turn. The thrower places his knees on the throwing line and may reach as far over the line as he chooses. He scores the number

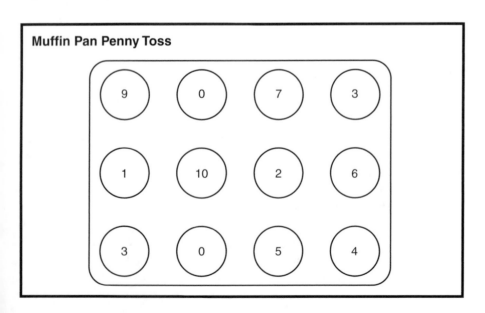

Muffin Pan Penny Toss

of points designated by the compartments of the pan in which his pennies rest. The player wins who makes 21 first.

Slipper Slap

This game is played with a slipper, or a piece of paper folded in several thicknesses to present a surface of about three by eight inches, firm but flexible. This may be crumpled at one end to form a sort of handle if desired.

A player is chosen to stand in the center. The others stand in a circle, shoulder-to-shoulder, so that the center player cannot see what goes on behind their backs. The players then pass the slipper from hand to hand behind their backs, taking every favorable opportunity to slap the one in the center with it, but the instant that this is done, the player holding the slipper must put it again behind her back and pass it to the next player, to avoid being caught with the slipper in her hand. The one in the center should try to catch any player who thus slaps her before the slipper is passed to another player.

Very rapid action and much sport may be had from this game. It is a rule to hit the center player with nothing but the slipper. The players will use any other feints they choose to mislead her as to who holds the slipper, pretending to pass it, or making a false move as though to hit her. The center player must catch one of the circle players with the slipper actually in her hands to have it count. Should this be done, she changes places with that player.

Couple Name Tag

To be played in a given area the size of a gym. Couples are in free formation with one couple appointed to be IT. All couples then select secret names. However, they must all be fish, birds, dogs, or another category that is given before the game starts. The couple that is IT walks through the group calling out names. When they guess one that was chosen by a couple, the couple has to run. Both couples must keep hands joined in chase. The game proceeds. However, hereafter the couple who isn't IT doesn't have to keep hands joined because there are two or more couple ITs chasing them. The game continues until everyone is caught or the names can't be guessed.

Attention Run

The group is divided into two teams of equal numbers. The teams are arranged in lines facing each other at a distance of 15 feet, the players in each group standing at normal intervals. Each team is numbered consecutively from left to right. The leader calls both groups to attention and soon thereafter calls a number within the limits of the numbers held by the participants. The two players holding this number step forward and run around to the right, each making a complete circle about his own line and returning to his original position. The other players assume "at rest" as soon as a number is called. The player standing at attention in his own position first, wins and scores one point for his team. The players are not allowed to touch the end members of their own team in turning corners. As soon as the first pair has finished, the leader calls both groups to attention again and calls a new number. This continues until all have run. The team scoring the most points wins.

Hole Ball

Each player digs a small hole in the ground two inches deep and four inches in diameter; all of the holes are massed in a group from four to six inches apart. If the game is played indoors, eight-inch squares may be chalked on the floor. A rolling line is established 20 feet from the holes. One player is the roller. He stands on the rolling line and starts with a soft ball. All of the other players (the runners) stand in back of the holes. At a signal, the roller rolls the ball so it will lodge in one of the holes. If it fails to drop in a hole, it is passed back to him; he continues to roll until the ball drops in a hole. When the ball settles in a hole, all the players but the owner of the hole the ball is in, run away. The owner of the hole the ball is in picks up the ball and throws it at the runners. Runners may attempt to dodge the ball. If a ball hits a runner, that player scores one dud and becomes the next roller. If the thrower fails to hit a runner, he scores one dud and becomes the roller. Throwers may not run with the ball. Pebbles or marks may be placed in each hole to keep score. After the ball is thrown it is recovered, all take their respective positions, and the game continues. Any player getting three duds has to pay a penalty.

Off the Spot

All but one of the group is arranged in a double circle so that no player is closer than 10 feet to another. Each player marks his position by using a large stone or by marking the floor. The extra player is IT and starts with a ball. At a signal, the players negotiate exchanges. IT attempts to hit one of the players with the ball while they are off their spot or when they step on an empty spot. Any player hit by the ball while off the spot or left without a spot becomes IT, and takes up the duties of that office immediately. IT is allowed to run with the ball as he desires.

Home Ball

The players stand scattered over the playing area. One player starts with a ball. At a signal, the player with the ball calls the name of another player. This player must stand still. The player with the ball throws it at him. If he is hit, he is eliminated. At the moment the ball leaves the thrower's hands, however, the person called may jump or run or do anything he wishes to avoid the ball. He may also attempt to catch the ball. If he fails, however, he is eliminated. On the other hand, if the player catches it, the thrower is eliminated. The player whose name was called, whether eliminated or not, recovers the ball and becomes the thrower. After throwing it, if he has been eliminated, he withdraws from the field. The thrower may not run with the ball, but may roll it along the ground and pick it up; he can then call a person's name and throw the ball. The elimination continues until all but one have withdrawn or been eliminated, this player is the winner.

Steal the Flag

The group is arranged in a circle, players standing at three foot intervals, facing in. One player is IT and stands in the center of the circle. Two flags (knotted towels) are placed within the circle next to IT. The players are numbered consecutively with IT having the highest number. At a signal, IT calls two numbers not greater than those held by the players. IT must always stand in the center of the circle when calling numbers. The players holding the numbers called must attempt to grab and fling one of the flags out of the circle before they are tagged by IT. Any player caught becomes IT. If IT fails to tag either player, he remains IT and calls two new numbers. If IT does succeed in tagging a player, he takes a position in the circle and the new IT comes to the center and calls two numbers. The game continues.

Punch Ball

All but one of the group is arranged in a single circle, players standing three feet apart, facing in. The extra player is IT and stands outside of the circle. One of the players in the circle starts with a ball. At a signal, the players in the circle pass the ball from one to another, attempting to keep the ball away from IT. IT runs about the circle attempting to punch the ball with his fist so it falls to the ground. The ball cannot be thrown across the circle, but must always be passed to the next player either on the right or the left. Any player (1) dropping the ball or (2) responsible for IT punching the ball so that it touches the ground becomes IT. The two exchange positions and the game continues.

Rushing the Spots

The group is arranged in a line at normal intervals. Each player but the leader marks a spot on the ground—chalk, a large stone, or a hat may be used. The players face to the right. At a signal, all run forward at a dog trot following the leader. The leader runs about the room as he chooses, forming spirals and circles.

At a signal (given by the leader or instructor), all break and run for spots, each player, including the leader, trying to get one not necessarily his own. As there is one more player than there are spots, one will be unsuccessful. This player scores one dud and takes the position at either end of the line as he chooses. At a signal, the players face right and follow the new leader at double time as before. At a signal, all break for the spots. This continues until one player has three duds. He must pay a penalty.

Waist Catch

All but two members of the group are in a double circle, facing in, the outside circle covering off the inside circle, each pair of players six feet apart. The players in the outside circle grasp the paired player in the inside circle around the waist. One of the two extra players is IT and the other is the runner. Both stand outside the circle. At a signal, IT chases the runner, attempting to tag him. The runner may make himself exempt from tagging by jumping in front of any of the players in the inside circle and having that player grasp him about the waist. When he does this he transfers his office to the rear player who then becomes the runner. The player in the rear may attempt to prevent the player in front from clasping the runner by turning him to one side or the other, hauling him forward or backward, or by any other fair tactics he may devise. When IT tags the player he is chasing, the two exchange offices and the game continues. The players must retain their circle formation.

Double Elimination Ball

The playing area is 50-feet square. Each person selects a partner. Then a playground ball or Nerf ball is thrown into the area. Any couple may pick it up and immediately throw it at other players. Any couple hit is eliminated. The game continues until all but one pair is eliminated. Players who are eliminated help throw in balls that go out of bounds.

Arch Bowls

Ten croquet arches are set up side-by-side, just far enough apart to allow the ball to pass through. A bowling line is marked 10 to 15 feet from the arches. Each player bowls one ball attempting to roll it through each arch in succession. The first arch must be made before the second and so on. A player plays until he misses. The first player through the 10 arches wins the game.

Prince of Paris

This is a very noisy game which requires little room but provides lots of excitement. The players are seated either in two rows facing each other or in a circle. The chairs are numbered, and the object of the game is for each player to get into the Number 1 chair and stay there as long as he can. The player's numbers change as they change chairs, and that's where the trouble is. Just as soon as a person gets it set in his mind that he is Number 3, he may have to move to chair Number 2. Someone calls out, "Number 2," before he collects his wits and off he has to go to the last seat. If a player forgets the number of the chair on which he is sitting, or to which he is advancing, he has to figure it out hurriedly as he moves about. There are no printed signs to help him. A player is chosen as leader; the others are numbered consecutively from one up and all are seated.

The leader standing in front says, "The Prince of Paris has lost his hat. Did you find it, Number 4, sir?" Whereupon Number 4 jumps to his feet and says: "What, sir! I, sir?"

Leader: "Yes, sir! You, sir!"

Number 4: "Not I, sir!"

Leader: "Who, then, sir?"

Number 4: "Number 7, sir!"

Number 7, as soon as his number is called, must jump at once to his feet and say, "What, sir! I, sir?"

Leader: "Yes, sir! You, sir!"

Number 7: "Not I, sir!"

Leader: "Who, then, sir?"

Number 7: "Number 3, sir!"

Number 3 immediately jumps to his feet, and the same dialogue is repeated. The object of the game is for the leader to try to repeat the statement, "The Prince of Paris has lost his hat," before the last player named can jump to his feet and say, "What, sir! I, sir?" If he succeeds in doing this, he changes places with the player failing in promptness, and that player becomes leader. Should any player fail to say *sir* in the proper place, this is also a mistake, and the leader may change places with such a player.

Games for the
Upper Grades

Artillery

The playing field should be 50-feet square with a "dead line" across the center of the field. A gymnasium works well. The group is divided into two teams of equal strength and they are scattered in the opposite halves of the field. At a signal, each captain throws a soft ball (playground or Nerf ball) at the players on the opposite team. Any player hit by the ball on the fly is eliminated and is therefore out of the game. Any player may catch the ball on the fly and not be eliminated. If he fails in his attempt, however, he is eliminated, and the ball becomes dead. Any ball caught on the fly eliminates the thrower. Dead balls are thereafter recovered by anyone and thrown at the players of the opposite team. In recovering or throwing a ball, players cannot cross the dead line. A ball out of bounds may be recovered by anyone, but must be thrown only from within bounds. Players hit or failing in an attempt to catch a ball withdraw from the field. This continues until one team has been completely eliminated; the surviving team is the winner.

Additional Comments:
- Multiple balls may be used with larger groups and for more action.
- This game is best played indoors, otherwise much time will be spent running down the balls.

Ball Passing

The playing field is 90-feet long by 50-feet wide. The group is divided into two teams of equal numbers. One team is marked so both teams are readily distinguished and both teams are scattered over the playing area. At a signal, the leader tosses the ball up in the center of the field between two players (one from each team). Either team acquiring the ball passes it about, attempting to make as many successive passes as possible—each pass scores one point. The score that counts, however, is not the total of passes made during the playing time but the score made during each separate instance that the team has the ball. If an opponent touches the ball it is considered lost. The team having the largest score of consecutive successive passes wins. A pass may be handed, rolled, or thrown in the air to count. The ball has merely to pass from a player to her teammate. If a foul is committed against a team while it is in possession of the ball, the count continues from the score it had when the foul was made. If a foul is committed by the team in possession, the ball is given to the other team. Either team forcing the ball out of bounds loses the ball as in basketball.

Additional Comments:
- The size of the playing field may be adjusted according to the number of players.
- The leader should review what constitutes a foul. The players and the leader may establish their own rules concerning fouls.

Basket Team Ball

Two basketball baskets are necessary for this game. The group is divided into two teams of equal numbers and placed in columns in back of the foul line which lies before each basket. The first player of each team is given a basketball. Twenty baskets constitute a game. A scorer is appointed for each team and placed a little distance from the basket. At a signal, the first player of each team shoots the ball at the basket. The second player rebounds it and shoots it. The other players follow in turn. Each player must get the ball without aid from his teammates and after shooting, whether scoring or failing, falls in at the end of his column. The scorer for each team, counting out loud, counts the baskets as they are made. When the last player of a team has made his shot the first player immediately follows. The game continues until one team has made 20 baskets. This team is then declared the winner.

Elimination Rope Pull

A rope 30-feet long with its end tied so it is endless is necessary for this game. The rope is placed on the ground so it forms a square. An object (e.g., stone, ball, or Indian club) is placed on the ground 10 feet from each corner of the rope. The players are arranged in a line at a little distance from the rope. The first four players take hold of the corners of the rope. At a signal, all pull, each attempting to reach and pick up the object lying at his corner. The player who succeeds is the winner—the other players are eliminated. The remaining players, pull in groups of four again. This continues until all but one has been eliminated; this player is the winner.

Bear in the Pit

All but one of the players are arranged in a circle, players facing in and holding hands. The extra player is the bear and stands in the center of the circle. At a signal, the bear attempts to break out of the circle, using all of the tactics that he can devise—crawling under, climbing over, or breaking through the players' held hands. Upon his getting out of the circle, the players release hands and chase him, attempting to catch and hold him for three seconds. The player who succeeds in catching the bear gets a free ride on the bear's back to the position of the circle. On reaching the starting position, the circle is re-formed, the player who rode the bear back becomes the bear and at a signal, the game continues.

Bodyguard Tag

The players are scattered over the playing area. One player is the chief and two others are guards. The two guards stand in front of the chief and join inside hands. At a signal, the runners attempt to tag the chief without being tagged themselves by the guards, it being the duty of the guards to attempt to tag the runners. Any runner tagged by either guard exchanges places with the guard. Any player tagging the chief becomes chief, which is the post of honor. The chief may move about the field as he wishes. The guards simply act as vassals and protect him. The members of the guards must retain their hand grasp and can only tag with the free hand. After each tag the game is halted until the players involved exchange places. When this change is completed the game is started again.

Boot the Pin

The group is divided into two teams of equal numbers. The two teams are arranged in separate circles 50 feet in diameter with an Indian club (the pin) in the center of each circle. One player in each circle starts with a ball (playground or soccer). Both teams should have the same kind of ball. At a signal, the players of each circle kick the ball, attempting to knock over the pin in the center, each hurrying to knock its own down first. The ball may be recovered from anywhere, but must be kicked at the pin only from the player's position in the circle. Players are not allowed to use hands at any time. The team that knocks down the pin first scores one point. After a point is scored, the game pauses. The club is set up again and the game starts again at a given signal. Ten points constitute a game.

Booting the Circle

The group is divided into two equal teams. One team is arranged in a circle facing out with players standing three feet apart. The second team is in a circle surrounding the first team and 20-feet distant from the same. The second team starts with a ball. At a signal, the players of the second (outside) team attempt to kick the ball inside the circle either by rolling it between the legs or throwing it between the players of the first (inside) team. The ball must go below the shoulders to score. The members of the outside team may approach the inside team to recover the ball, but must kick it at the distance of not less than 20 feet from the circle. The players forming the inside circle may use their hands in defense. When the ball enters the inside circle, the two teams change positions and the game continues.

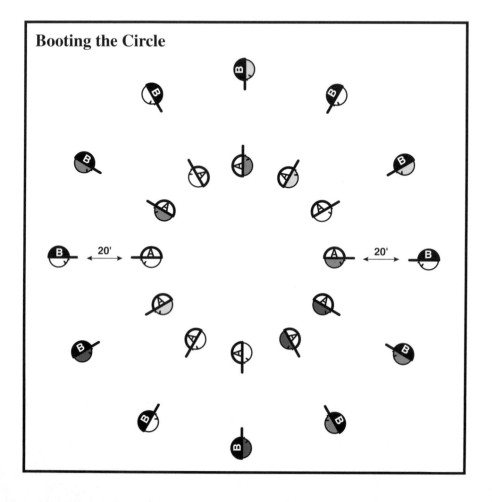

Booting the Circle

Additional Comments:
- Instead of changing positions each time the ball enters the circle, a time limit may be set and the score counted in that time. The most scores win.

Bounce Ball

A well-defined playing area 50-feet long by 40-feet wide is required. The field is divided into two 20-by-50-foot courts. The group is divided into two teams of even numbers. Each team is divided in half and one half of each team is assigned to one of the two courts. The other half of each team stands in back of the opponent's baseline. In their proper positions the teams will stand as follows: Baseline Group A, Center Group B, Center Group A, and Baseline Group B. One of the Center Group A players starts the game with a ball that will bounce (e.g., basketball, volleyball or playground ball). Upon a signal, the player

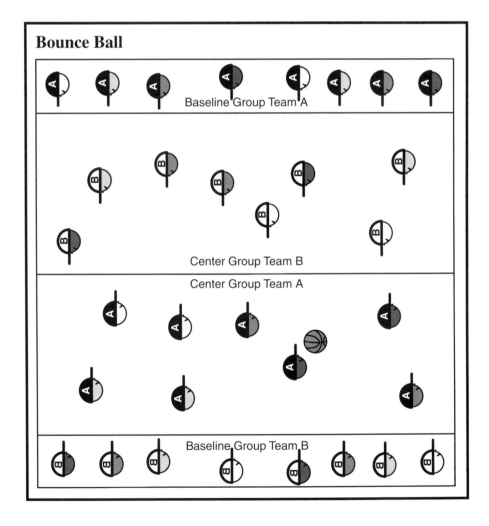

Bounce Ball

Baseline Group Team A

Center Group Team B

Center Group Team A

Baseline Group Team B

with the ball attempts to hit one of the Center Group B players of Team B. Any player of the group hit in this manner is eliminated and should withdraw from the field of play at once. If the ball fails to hit a player on Team B and goes through to Baseline Group A, anyone of that group may recover it and attempt again to eliminate players of Center Group B. If the ball fails to hit a player and is also not caught by a member of the Center Group A, but goes through to Baseline Group B, and then this group may recover it and try to eliminate players in Center Group A. Only the baseline players can recover the ball out of bounds, and they must throw only from the baseline. When the ball goes out of bounds, it belongs to the side which recovers it. A ball hitting a center group player on the floor after the first bounce does not eliminate the player—fair hits are made on one bounce only. The elimination continues until all of one center group is eliminated. The other team wins.

Bounce Tag Ball

The playing area is 50-feet square and the players are scattered over the playing area. Two players are IT and each has a baton. The other players have one ball (e.g., basketball, volleyball, or playground ball). At a signal, the two ITs working independently, run for the ball, attempting to tag it. The tag should be made with the baton. The other players pass the ball around as they please, but each player upon receiving it must bounce it at least once in place before throwing it. The players are not allowed to run with the ball. Any player catching the ball while running must halt immediately. Any player responsible for either IT touching the ball becomes IT. The IT who touches the ball gives his baton to the new IT, joins the runners, and the game continues.

Bounce Net Ball

On a volleyball court, the group is divided into two teams of equal numbers and scattered on opposite sides of the net. Team A starts with a ball. At a signal, Team A bounces the ball on the floor on its own side of the net so it flies over the net. Team B receives the ball, bounces it as hard on the floor as the players wish among themselves and then Team A receives it and bouncing it in the same manner returns it again. The ball is passed back and forth across the net until one team commits a foul. A team may return the ball across the net any time it wishes to. No player is allowed to bounce the ball more than once from the time it is received by his team until the time it is returned to the opponents. The ball is never volleyed as in volleyball, but always bounced on the floor. If either team fails to return the ball fairly (i.e., commits a foul by catching the ball, knocking it out of bounds, touching the net, having a player hit it more than once on a service, or volleying the ball at any time instead of bouncing it), one point is scored for the opposing team. The ball is put into play after every score by the team making the point. Fifteen points constitute a game.

Bounce Volleyball

On a volleyball court, the group is divided into two teams of equal numbers and each is scattered on opposite sides of the net. Team A starts with a ball. At a signal, Team A serves the ball across the net. Team B must let the ball strike the ground once and then knock it back across the net. Then Team A lets the ball strike the ground once and knocks it back. Either team may hit the ball as much as it wishes before letting it bounce, but must hit it across the net immediately after doing so with no further bouncing or hitting. If either team fails to return the ball fairly (i.e., commits a foul by allowing it to hit the floor more than once, hitting it more than once after it strikes the floor, knocking it out of bounds, catching it, touching the net, or failing to let the ball hit the floor), one point is scored by the opposing team. The ball is put in play after every score by the team making the point. Fifteen points makes the game.

Break the Fence

The group stands in a single circle, facing in, players holding hands. Two players are bulls and stand in the center of the circle. At a signal, the bulls attempt to break out of the circle by charging the hands of the players. It is unlawful for both bulls to charge the same point at the same time. When either bull breaks out, the two players responsible each score a dud and become bulls in place of the two previously appointed. The first bulls take positions in the circle. The new bulls attempt to break out. In this way the game continues until a player has three duds. This player must pay a forfeit of the group's choosing.

Deck Tennis

In this game two or four players toss a rope ring back and forth over the net, which should be four feet above the ground at the middle of an 18-by-40-foot court. Rope rings may be purchased, or three may be made from a four-foot piece of manila rope. The official ring is six inches in diameter and one-half-inch thick.

The choice of service or court is decided by the toss of a coin. The object of the game is to toss the ring over the net into the opponent's court so that it hits the ground or floor before the opponent can catch it. The game is usually 15 points, with a set of two permitted at 14-all. A player loses the point if the ring lands in his own court of if he throws the ring outside the opponent's court.

The players catch the ring with one hand only and return it immediately upon being caught, with the same hand and from the spot where it is caught—

no holding it, stepping with it, feinting, batting, or juggling it. The players must toss the ring underhand or horizontally. It cannot be thrown down with an overhand motion. The players may not raise their elbows above their shoulders unless the ring has been caught above them. In this case, they may return the ring from the height where caught, provided that only a tossing motion of the wrist is employed. Only one player on a team may touch the ring during the same play. The first player must stand behind his right-hand court and serve to the court diagonally opposite. If he scores a point, he then serves from behind his left-hand court into the court diagonally opposite, or the opponent's left-hand court. Only the server scores. He continues to serve as long as he makes points.

Captain Center Ball

The group is divided into two teams of equal number. One team forms a circle 40 feet in diameter. The other team forms in a circle around the first team, each player covering off a player of the inside circle. The players making up each alternate pair exchange places (see illustration). This makes an arrangement where the players of each team alternate in both the front and rear ranks. Two circles three feet in diameter and six feet apart are marked in the center of the circles. One player of each team is chosen captain and placed on one of these spots. Two other players are selected as guards and placed beside the opposing team's captain. One of the players in the circle has a ball.

At a signal, the game starts. The players on Team A try to pass the ball to their captain. The players on Team B try to pass to their captain. The guards try to prevent the opposing captains from getting the ball. They may move anywhere they choose. On securing the ball, they may not pass it to their own team captains, but pass it to their teammates in the circle. The captains must keep one foot on their respective spots. Each attempts to get the ball as it is passed to him. If the ball goes outside of the circle the players in the rear rank recover it. It then belongs to the player who gets it first. This player may try to toss it to his captain. The players of the front rank in the circle must retain their positions at all times. The players in the outside circle must not interfere with the players in the inside circle. Each time a Captain gets the ball one point is scored for his team. After each point the players of the inside circle and outside circle change positions. Ten points constitute a game.

POW (Prisoner of War)

The playing area is 20 feet by 40 feet. The lines on the long side of the playing area are the baselines. The lines on the short sides are the end lines. The group is divided into two teams of equal number. One team is marked well so both teams are easily distinguished. The teams stand directly in front of opposite

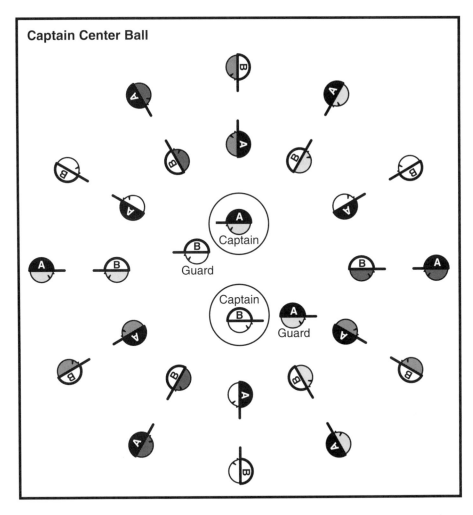

Captain Center Ball

baselines, facing each other. At a signal, each team rushes forward and attempts to pull, drag, or carry opponents back across its baseline. A player is not allowed to take refuge behind his own baseline or to step over the end lines; any player doing either of these things commits a foul and is expelled from the game. Players pulled completely over their opponent's baselines are required to stay behind that line. Any tactics which are not abusive are permissible. Any number may combine to attack a lone opponent. The team that completely eliminates its opponents wins.

Additional Comments:
- This game can also be played with the players in a kneeling position rather than standing. This may be preferable for older children as the game may not get as rough. However, the leader should make sure all

players remove their shoes before the game starts. The players must also keep their knees on the ground when attacking or escaping.

Cat Tail

The group is arranged in a single line, players standing at normal intervals. The leader will locate the center player in the line. This player is the pivot. The group on one side of the pivot represents one team; the group on the other side another team. The teams face in opposite directions. Then all of the players of both teams join hands, inside players of both teams linking hands with the pivot player. At a signal, both teams, retaining their hand grasps, run forward in a circle about the pivot. The race continues until the outside player of one team reaches and tags the outside player of the other team. The team succeeding in doing this wins. If either team breaks, victory is forfeited to the opposing team.

Catch and Throw

The playing area is a rectangular field, 60-feet square. The players stand behind one of the end lines. One player is IT and she stands in the center of the field. At a signal, the players behind the line run for the opposite line. IT attempts to prevent their reaching the line by catching and wrestling them to the floor. Any player forced in any way to touch the floor with any part of the body other than her feet is eliminated and becomes IT, joining the old IT in the center of the field. After the players have all reached the opposite line or have joined IT, the signal is given again and the players attempt to recross. The ITs, both the old and the new, as before, catch and wrestle all the runners they can. Those wrestled to the floor join IT. The players run back and forth in this manner until all are caught. The last player caught is the champion or is IT for the next game.

Center Club Bowl

The group is arranged in a circle 40 feet in diameter. The players count off. The odds constitute one team, the evens constitute another. The leader places an Indian club standing upright in the center of the circle and gives one of the players a ball. At a signal, the player with the ball, standing in his position, bowls it at the Indian club, attempting to knock it over. Each player in turn, continuing from the bowler's right, then makes one attempt. After each throw the ball is recovered by anyone and given to the next bowler. Each player who knocks over the club scores one point for his team. The club is set up each time it is knocked over. The team scoring the greatest number of points wins.

Chain Hop Elimination

The group is arranged in a single column at normal intervals. Each player raises his right foot backward, grasps the raised foot of the player in front of him with his right hand, and places his left hand on the same player's shoulder. At a signal, all hop forward on the left foot, continuing forward until a gap has been created. The player losing his grip on the player in front is eliminated and withdraws to one side. The players in the column release their grasps, face about, and assume the starting position and on signal move forward in the opposite direction until another gap appears. The player responsible withdraws; the column reunites and advances again. This continues until another gap appears. The player responsible withdraws, the column reunites and advances again. This continues until two players remain in the column; they are both recognized as the winners. The players should face about after each elimination.

Circle Boot Ball

All but one of the group is arranged in a circle, facing in, players holding hands and standing two feet apart. The extra player is IT and stands in the center of the circle. At a signal, IT attempts to kick a ball through the circle. The ball must either pass through the legs or between the members (not higher than the shoulders) forming the circle to constitute a fair out. The players forming the circle may use their joined hands and their legs to prevent the ball going out. If the ball goes over the heads of the players in the circle it is recovered, brought to the center, and play starts again. When the ball penetrates the circle, the player responsible becomes IT. The old and new IT exchange places and the game continues.

Circle Race (Miss 'n' Out)

A circular track 60 yards in circumference or the perimeter of a gym is designated the playing area. The players arrange themselves about the track equal distances apart. At a signal, each player runs forward with the object of catching up to and tagging the runners in front, and incidentally, avoiding being so caught and tagged himself. Runners tagged drop out of the race; the tagger in each case continues forward to eliminate other runners. The race continues until all but one player has been eliminated. This runner is the winner.

Variations:
- For Miss 'n' Out all the players race together. At the finish line of each lap, the person in last place is eliminated. The race continues until all but one player has been eliminated.

Make Me Laugh

Two teams line up shoulder-to-shoulder facing each other about 20 feet apart. The leader chooses one player from Team A. That player walks over to any player from Team B and has 30 (or 45 or 60) seconds to make that person laugh (the leader may determine what constitutes a laugh—broad smile or stifled giggle). The player from Team A, may sing, make faces, fall down on the ground, or anything judged socially appropriate by the leader and the group to make the other player laugh, however, he may not touch that player. The player on the receiving end must maintain eye contact with the player trying to make him laugh. If the player from Team A can make the other player laugh, the laugher is out of the game. If the player from Team A is unsuccessful, then he is out of the game. Now it is Team B's turn. The game continues until one team has been eliminated.

Club Chase

The leader will establish two lines 30-feet long, 30 feet apart. The group is divided into sections of eight players each and each section stands in a line behind one of the baselines. Seven Indian clubs are placed in a row about four

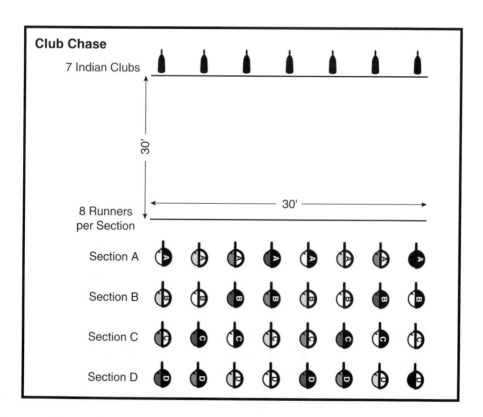

feet apart on the opposite baseline. At a signal, the first section runs for the clubs, each player trying to get a club. As there is one club less than the number of runners, one player fails to get a club, and this player is eliminated. The clubs are set back in place and the next section runs. This continues until each section has run. All but the losers then return to their original positions. There are now seven in each section. One club is removed and the sections run as before, the losers being eliminated. This continues until there is but one left in each section. The section winners are then assembled at the starting line in one group, clubs are set on the opposite line (one less than the number of runners) and the elimination continues until one player is left. This player is the winner.

Club Guard

All but one of the players is in a circle 35 feet in diameter, facing in. Three Indian clubs are placed three feet apart so they form a triangle in the center of the circle. The extra player is the guard and stands in the center of the circle. The players in the circle have a ball. At a signal, the player having the ball kicks it toward the clubs, attempting to knock one of them over. After the game has started, players may use only their feet. Players may recover the ball, both outside and inside of the circle, but can only kick it at the clubs from their respective positions in the circle. Any player causing a club to fall over, either by knocking it over directly with a fairly kicked ball or causing the guard to knock it over, becomes the guard. The old guard takes position in the circle, the new guard sets up the club and the game continues.

Crocodile Chase

This game requires two pieces of rope 25-feet long. The group is divided into two teams. Each team stands in a column and each team has one of the ropes which the players hold in the left hand. At a signal, the head of each column chases the tail of the other. The team whose head player succeeds in tagging the tail player of the opposing team first wins.

Dog and Cat

All but two of the players are arranged in a circle, standing four feet apart and facing in. One of the selected players is the dog and the other is the cat. They stand on opposite sides of the circle. At a signal, the dog chases the cat. The cat may run between any of the open gaps between the players, but as soon as he has, the gap becomes closed and he cannot thereafter run through it again. To close a gap the two players standing adjacent to the gap through which the cat has run, grasp hands at shoulder height. The dog, on the other hand, can only run through the closed gaps; he must duck under the raised hands. The game continues until the cat is caught. Two new players are then appointed dog and cat. The previous runners join the circle and at a signal, the game continues.

King of the Cage

The well-defined playing area is 20-feet square. All of the players are inside of the area. At a signal, each player attempts to force the other players out of the square. Each player against all others. Players may use any tactics they wish, except any unnecessary roughness such as striking or kicking. Any player touching any part of the body outside of the square is eliminated and withdraws from the playing area. This continues until one player remains. This player is the winner and crowned King of the cage.

Corner Ball

The playing field is 40 feet by 60 feet with a line dividing the field in half so as to make two 30-by-40-feet courts. The four corner areas are six-feet square. The group is divided into two teams. Team A is scatter over one half of the field and Team B is scattered over the other half. Two players from Team A stand in the back corners of Team B (one in each corner) and two players on Team B stand in the back corners of Team A's territory. The teams are not allowed to cross the center line. The corner players are required to stay in their corner areas, and their opponents are not allowed to step into these areas. Any

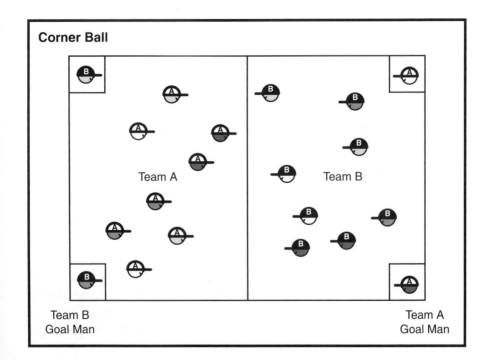

player stepping into the corner area scores a point for the opposing team. The leader starts the game by tossing the ball up between two players in the center. Each team tries to pass the ball to its corner players. Every time a corner player catches the ball one point is scored for his team. The game continues after every score with the corner player passing the ball to the opposing team. The team having the most points at the end of five minutes wins.

Additional Comments:
  • The leader should teach his group to play End Ball before playing Corner Ball. Teaching suggestions are included with the description of End Ball.

Double Tag

The playing area is 40-feet square. The group is arranged in pairs and placed, all but one pair, in scattered positions outside the playing area. The two selected players are IT. They start in the center of the playing area and have their elbows linked. At a signal, the other players enter the field and tantalize the ITs who chase them and attempt to tag them. These players do not link their elbows but run about independently. Any player tagged by either IT in the playing area is caught and must take up a position in the center of the field. A tag made while the ITs are unlinked is null. Any player leaving the playing area after the game has begun is considered caught. The ITs continue their chase until both players of a pair have been tagged. This pair then becomes IT. The other players return to the outside of the playing area and at a signal, the game is restarted.

Drill Elimination

The group is in an open formation. The leader calls the group to attention and gives any marching or calisthenics commands that the players are familiar with. Those who fail to execute the proper movements on the first trial are eliminated. Those who are eliminated may sit on the floor. The leader will continue giving commands, gradually increasing difficulty, until all are down. The last player eliminated is the champion.

Five Duds

The group is arranged in a circle, with players three feet apart. The group counts off with the odds making up one team and the evens another. The players of one team are marked to distinguish teams. This game requires two balls that differ in size or color, and each team has one. At a signal, each team passes its ball about as the members choose. Each player must pass the ball as soon as he receives it. Either team dropping the ball immediately scatters. The player of the other team holding the ball at this moment, attempts to hit one of them. If he succeeds, one dud is scored for that team (the team hit), if he fails no score is made. Both teams re-form and the game is started again. The game continues until one team scores five duds. All of the members of that team must pay a penalty at the end of each game.

End Ball

This game is played with a basketball, volleyball, or a playground ball. The players form two teams. One third of the players on each team are end men and the others are guards. The object of the game is for a guard to throw the ball over the heads of the opposing guards to one of his own end men while the end player has both feet in his end area (see diagram). A point is earned for each successful pass. The game may be played in three- to five-minute halves with one- to two-minute rest periods between halves.

The diagram shows 12 players on each team; this is a good number for an interesting game. The size of the court will depend upon the abilities of the players. A regulation basketball court with end areas inside the rear boundary lines is usually suitable.

The game is started with a tossup between the opponents who have come to the center; one player stands on each side of the center line and each player attempts to bat the ball to his own guards. Play is continuous. When an end player receives the ball, he immediately throws the ball back to his guards. A guard may pass the ball to another guard or attempt to score with a throw to his end player. A ball which goes out of bounds is recovered by a nearby player, brought inside the boundary line at the point where it went out, and put into play again.

It is a foul for a guard to step across the center line or into the opponents' end area. The ball is given to the nearest opponent when a foul is committed. The team that scores the highest number of points within the playing time wins the game.

Additional Comments:
- The leader should teach quick passing, accurate catching, distance throwing, and guarding and intercepting throws.
- The players should rotate so that all team members play different positions on the floor.
- This game may be played with many balls and/or Frisbees for faster action. A variety of balls (e.g., playground, Wiffle, and footballs) will enhance throwing and catching skills.
- It is best to have at least one leader recording the score for each team. When multiple balls are used, scoring becomes fast and furious.

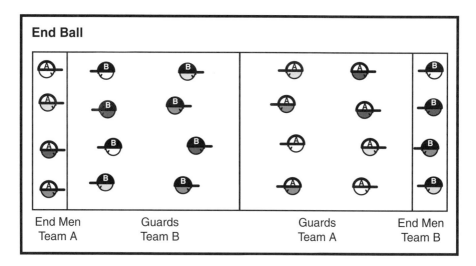

End Ball

End Men Team A	Guards Team B	Guards Team A	End Men Team B

Foot Tag Ball

All but one of the group is arranged in a circle 40 feet in diameter, players facing in. The extra player is IT and stands in the center of the circle. One of the players standing in the circle starts with a ball. At a signal, the players in the circle kick the ball about, attempting to prevent IT from kicking it. IT attempts to kick the ball. Players may stop the ball with their body and hands, but may not catch or bat it. Any player who is responsible for IT touching the ball, is responsible for the ball going out of the circle, or catches or bats the ball with his hands becomes IT. The old and new ITs exchange places and, at a signal, the game continues.

High Touch Elimination

A ball is attached to a small 20-foot-long rope and the rope is hung over a beam or limb of a tree. The ball and rope are adjusted so that the ball is at a height of seven feet. A springboard is placed before the ball. The players are arranged in a column 20 feet from the springboard. At a signal, the column slowly moves forward. Each player in turn jumps from the springboard and attempts to touch the ball with his hand. The ball should be restored to a quiet position after each touch. Those players who fail to touch are eliminated. Those who succeed fall into column in their original positions. The ball is elevated for each round and the game continues until all are eliminated, the last one being the winner.

Additional Comments:
- The leader should make sure appropriate equipment is available to land safely.

Goal Kick Ball

Two well-defined 30-by-15 feet rectangles are established on the ends of the playing field. The group is divided into two teams and each team is scattered on opposite halves of the field facing the center; the rectangle in back of each team is that team's goal. Team A starts with a ball (soccer or rugby). The leader will designate the style of kicking (punt, drop, or place) before play begins. At a signal, one of the players on Team A, standing on the starting line, kicks the ball in the designated manner toward Team B's goal. If the ball is not caught, it is kicked from the point where it was first touched by the player who first touched it. The ball is kicked back and forth, always in the designated manner, each team attempting to kick it in the opposite area. Violation of lines (entering the goal area) scores a point for the opponents. A point is scored each time the ball hits the goal from the starting line by the team scored against. If the ball is kicked over the goal, it is kicked back from the center of the front line of the goal. Five points constitute a game and the team scoring this number first wins.

Hobo

All of the group except one player is arranged in a circle or rectangle, players standing 10 feet apart, facing in. The extra player (the hobo) stands in the center of the circle. Each player marks the place where he is standing, using stones, chalk, or tape. At a signal, the players seek to exchange positions. The hobo attempts to get into one of the vacated positions. All of the players help the hobo by attempting to deceive their fellow players by negotiating an exchange, starting to carry it out, and then returning to their starting position. When the hobo secures a place, all of the players seek a place and hold it. The player without a position is then the hobo. The game continues.

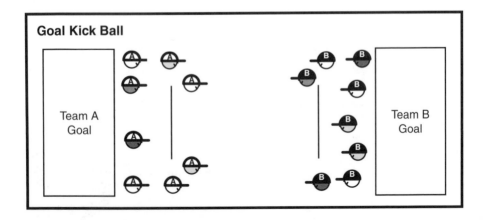

Hop Tag

A circle, three feet in diameter, is drawn in the center of the playing area. One player is IT and stands in the circle. Here he may stand on both feet. At a signal, IT, hopping on one foot, chases the other players, attempting to tag one. If, after leaving his base, he touches the other foot to the floor, he must return to the base to make himself well to tag. The other players may touch him with their open hands without being tagged while he is doing this. While IT is hopping on one foot the other players may try to overbalance him but they make themselves liable to tagging. Any player tagged becomes IT.

Circle Hop Tag

All but one of the players is arranged in a circle 35 feet in diameter, with players facing in. The extra player is IT and stands in the center of the circle. The players are numbered consecutively, with IT being the last number. At a signal, IT, standing on one leg, calls three numbers. She must stand in the center while calling. The players holding the numbers called run and attempt to exchange places. IT attempts to get into one of the places; in making the attempt she is required to hop. If IT fails to get a place, she remains IT and calls three new numbers. If she succeeds, the expelled player becomes IT, and the game continues.

Hopping Circle

All but one of the group is arranged in a circle, with players standing about four feet apart, facing in, and holding hands. The extra player is given a light rope about 15-feet long with a soft weight at one end. At a signal, he swings the rope about, close to the ground so the weight travels just inside the circle of players. As soon as the weight is traveling he calls, "Hop!" At this signal, all of the players lift one foot from the floor and begin to hop over the rope which the player in the center lets swing a trifle wider. Any player who releases hands with his neighbor, puts his lifted foot on the ground, or fails to jump the rope (stops it) is given one dud. After each dud, the center player swings the rope as in the beginning. Any player scoring three duds must pay a penalty.

Hop Toad

The group is arranged in a circle 30 feet in diameter, players squatting six feet apart and facing to the left. One player stands in the center, with a light rope about 20-feet long with a weight at one end. At a signal, he swings the rope around close to the ground, so it reaches the players in the circle. Each player, as the rope approaches him, executes a short quadruple dive over the rope; that is, jumping off his feet so as to assume a squatting position. Players who stop the rope are eliminated and withdraw. The last player forced out is champion.

Horse and Rider Rope Pull

This game requires a rope one-and-one-half inches in diameter and 60-feet long. The rope is stretched across a level piece of ground. The center of the rope and the ground over which the center rests are marked. The group is divided into two teams and placed at opposite ends of the rope. Each team is arranged in pairs, horses and riders. The riders mount the horses' shoulders and hold the rope. The leader should set a time limit of 30 or 60 seconds. At a signal, each team pulls the rope, attempting to pull the opponents across the center line. Any rider falling to the ground must release his grasp on the rope until he has remounted. The leader calls time at the end of the specified period. The team having the center of the rope on its side wins.

Hunter and Hunted

All but three of the group are arranged in a circle, players holding hands at shoulder height. The three players are numbered one, two, three, and placed equal distance apart outside of the circle. At a signal, one chases two, two chases three, and three chases one. Each tries to tag the person ahead of him and keep from being caught. Runners may run in and out about the circle but must not go more than 10 feet beyond the outside of the circle. The players in the circle are not allowed to interfere with the runners. The chase continues until one player has been tagged. This player is eliminated. The next three runners then step out of the circle and the three who have just run take their places. The game continues until all have run. The winners are numbered off again, a new round is played, and winners decided. The last player left is the winner.

Hurry Ball

All but one of the group is arranged in a circle 15 feet in diameter. The extra player is IT. IT has a ball (playground or tennis) and stands in the center. At a signal, IT tosses the ball into the air to a height of 15 feet so it will drop in the center. As the ball descends IT either catches it or lets it drop to the floor. If she catches it, she attempts to tag one of the players with it before they can sit on the floor and raise their feet. If IT lets the ball drop to the floor, the players are not required to sit on the floor and they cannot be tagged. A touched ball is considered caught. Any player who makes a move to sit down is eligible to have the ball thrown at her by IT as soon as IT recovers the ball. As soon as a player discovers her mistake, she may run away from IT. Any player hit by the ball thrown by IT exchanges places.

Imitation Tag

This game is played as tag with the exception that the player who is IT may choose the style of travel (e.g., one foot, double jumping, walking, running, frog jumping, or duck waddling). When a player becomes IT, he takes up the style of travel he desires, and the rest must conform. Any player who does not conform becomes IT, as well as any player who runs out of bounds.

In and Out

One player starts with a light rope 20-feet long with a weight at one end. She stands in the center of the playing area. The other players are arranged in a column 30 feet from the player with the rope. The player with the rope swings it so that it circles slowly around close to the ground. At a signal, the column slowly moves forward, and each player in turn runs into the area of the circling rope, touches the player swinging the rope and runs out. Players may not jump the rope and may leave the area at any point they wish. Players who touch or hold the rope are eliminated. Those who succeed in touching the player with the rope re-form in a new column. This time the rope is swung more rapidly and those failing withdraw, those succeeding re-form in a column until all are eliminated. The last player eliminated is champion.

Individual Basketball

This game is played on a basketball court. The group counts off. Player 1 starts with a basketball and stands on the foul line. At a signal, he attempts to throw a basket. If he fails, Player 2 catches the ball and attempts to throw from where he recovers the ball. The game continues in this manner. After a successful throw, the next player throws from the foul line. Any player holding the ball over five seconds forfeits his chance. Five points constitute a game.

Individual Dodge Ball

All but one member of the group is arranged in a circle 25 feet in diameter, players facing in. The extra player stands in the center. One player starts with a ball. At a signal, this player throws the ball at the center player. The center player tries to avoid being hit. If the throw is unsuccessful the ball is recovered and rethrown. Any player in the circle may recover it. All throws must be made from the thrower's position on the circle. This continues until the center player is hit. Every throw at him scores one point for him. When he is hit, he takes a position in the circle and another player from the circle takes position in the center. The player scoring the largest number of points wins.

Individual Dud Ball

The playing area is 80-feet square. The players are assembled in the center of the playing area. One player is the runner and starts with a ball (playground, volleyball, or basketball). At a signal, the runner tosses the ball straight up in the air and runs, attempting to keep away from the ball. One of the other players catches the ball and passes it to another. Thereafter, players may run about as they choose, but may not carry the ball. A player, on receiving the ball, must halt and remain in place until he has passed it or thrown it at the runner. Any player responsible for the ball touching the ground after the original toss receives one dud. The game continues until a player has three duds. This player is compelled to pay a penalty.

Frisbee Golf

The leader and players may set up their own course outdoors (or even indoors). The object is to throw the Frisbee and hit a specific target. Each hole should be varied in distance and difficulty. This can be played as individuals, teams, or even as a tournament or in leagues.

Individual Soccer

The group is divided into two teams of equal numbers. The teams are arranged facing each other along parallel lines 30 feet apart with the players standing with feet spread so each touches those of his neighbors. The players also hold

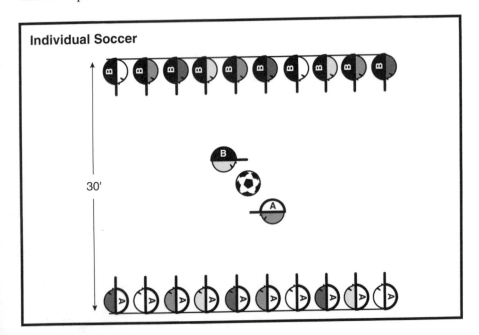

Individual Soccer

30'

hands. A ball is placed in the center of the field. At a signal, the first player from each team runs forward and attempts to kick the ball through the opponents' line. Kicking the ball through the line scores one point. To pass a line fairly, the ball must pass within the limits of the two ends of each team and below the heads of the players. The players in the line may use all parts of the body in blocking the ball, but one foot must always be kept on the line and the hands must be kept joined. Either team stepping off the line, breaking hands, or allowing the ball to pass through their ranks scores one point for the opponents. Either team kicking the ball across the opponents' line unfairly (over heads or offside) scores one point for the opponents. The ball is replaced in the center after each point and the next two players take up the contest. This continues until all have one chance. The high scoring team wins.

Island Tag

Mats are arranged about the gym floor. The floor is the sea; the mats are the islands. The players are scattered about the floor. One player is IT and another is the helper. At a signal, IT chases the other players, attempting to tag one. Players standing on islands are free from tagging. The helper aids IT by pushing players off of the islands into the sea. In doing this he may only push and charge players, he may not hold them with his arms. Any player fairly tagged by IT becomes IT. The old IT then becomes the helper and the old helper joins the players. A player touching the floor in any way can be tagged.

Jump Stick Elimination

The players are arranged in a column, players standing three feet apart. Two players stand 10 feet in front of the column holding a six-foot stick at right angles to the column and about a foot off the ground. At a signal, the players with the stick run back toward the front of the column, one going on each side so the players in the column have to jump the stick. Any player failing to jump the stick withdraws. Reaching the back of the column, the runners and the players in the column turn about, and the runners carry the stick back down the column. The stick is raised about three inches. The last player eliminated is champion.

Jump the Shoe

All but one of the group is arranged in a circle 30 feet in diameter. The circle is divided into two teams of equal numbers. The players on each team are numbered consecutively from right to left. One player is in the center of the circle, and she has a light rope about 15-feet long with a soft flat object like a shoe tied at one end. At a signal, she swings the rope around in a circle so that the shoe slides along the floor about three feet in front of the players. The rope should be swung at a speed that accords with the skill of the players. At a signal, Player 1 of each team attempts to jump on the shoe. All jumps must be made from the jumper's position in the circle, jumping with both feet together. The player who jumps on the shoe and remains on it first scores one point for her team. If either player jumps on the rope or in front of the shoe or rope and fails to get out of its way, thereby halting it, one point is scored for the opposite team. After each attempt that does not score a point, the player must return to her position and try again when the shoe comes around. After a point is scored the shoe is swung again and at a signal, Players 2 from each team make their attempts. Players 3 follow, and so on, until all have tried. The team scoring the largest number of points wins.

Leader and Footer

All but two members of the group are arranged in a column. The first player of the column is the leader and the last is the footer. The two other players stand 30 feet apart, directly in front of the column. Each leans forward and puts his hands on his knees. They are known as backs. At a signal, the footer directs the method through which the distance between the two backs should be traveled. The leader and all behind him in turn straddle vault the first back and attempt to clear the space to the second back in the prescribed manner and then straddle over the second back. Any player failing becomes second back. Second back becomes first back; first back takes position in front of leader thereby becoming leader. The game continues. When all have completed the attempt, the footer sets a new challenge. The leader may challenge the request of the footer at any time, and then the footer must make the attempt first. If he succeeds, the leader becomes second back and all of the other players have to try it. The other players change accordingly. If he fails, he becomes second back and no one else has to attempt it; the player at the end of the column then becomes footer and gives a new order. Examples of methods for clearing the space are hop on one foot, five hops, four hops, four double jumps, two hops, two steps and two jumps, and hop-step-jump.

Leap the Brook

The playing court is 60 feet by 30 feet. The long sides are the baselines, the short sides the sidelines. Two lines are drawn running parallel to the baselines in the center of the court which while running practically parallel curve slightly, so at different places they are six, eight, ten, and twelve feet apart. The space between the two lines is the brook. All but two of the players start on the baseline. The two ITs are placed in the brook. At a signal, all players on the baseline run forward, attempting to jump the brook and reach the other baseline without

Leap the Brook

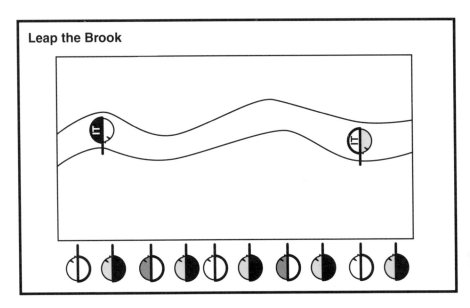

being tagged by the ITs who must remain in the brook. Any player tagged by either IT becomes IT and the player who tagged him is eliminated and withdraws from the field. A tag made while the tagger is outside the brook is null. Any player stepping in the brook is eliminated. When all have been tagged or have reached the further baseline, a new signal is given and the players attempt to return to the opposite baseline, advancing under previous conditions. After each signal, players are given 15 seconds to cross the brook. Those who are not over in this period are eliminated. The players run back and forth in this manner until all are eliminated. The last player eliminated is the winner.

Leg Dive Tag

All of the group but two are arranged in a circle 30 feet in diameter. All the players in the circle spread their legs. Of the selected players, one is IT and the other is the runner. They start on opposite sides of the circle. At a signal, IT chases the runner. The runner moves about and suddenly dives between the spread legs of one of the players in the circle. This player then becomes the runner. The old runner takes the new runner's place in the circle, but stands with feet together; legs are spread at a signal. The method of play prevents a few players from monopolizing the game.

Line Ball

The throwing lines are two parallel lines 60 feet apart. The standing line is a third line halfway between and parallel to the throwing lines. All but two of the players stand at normal intervals in a column on the standing line. Each of the two players on the throwing line starts with a ball. At a signal, these players throw the balls simultaneously at the center players in such a manner that the ball will hit one or more of them on the first bounce. The balls may be thrown from any position on the throwing line. The players on the standing line may dodge and twist and jump as they see fit to evade the balls, but they must keep on the line. Any player fairly hit is eliminated and takes the position of the player who hit him, this player (the thrower) withdraws altogether. After each hit the column closes its ranks to normal distances. After each throw the balls are recovered by the throwers, be they new or old, and thrown again. This continues until all have been eliminated. The last player eliminated is the champion.

Line Captain Ball

The group is divided into two teams of equal numbers. All but one member of each team are in parallel lines 50 feet apart, players facing in. A spot three feet in diameter is established halfway between the opposing lines. The two selected players alternately serve as captain and guard. To start, the players of Team A are given a ball and the captain of Team A stands on the spot. The captain of Team B acts as guard. At a signal, the player holding the ball attempts to pass it to his captain. The captain must keep one foot on the spot. The guard tries to prevent the captain from getting the ball in any way he can, so long as he does not step in the circle. Stepping in the circle scores one point for the captain. If the captain secures the ball, one point is scored for his team. If the guard secures it, he tosses it to his team and takes a position on the spot as captain. The captain of Team A then becomes guard. After each point two new captains are appointed. Ten points constitute a game.

Mass Basketball

This game is played as the regular game of basketball with the following exceptions:

1. a large number is allowed to play;
2. there is no halftime;
3. all fouls eliminate the person committing them;
4. after a foul the ball is tossed into the air between two players of the opposite team at the point where the foul was made;
5. boundary lines are not recognized—in other words, the ball is never out of bounds—and
6. five minutes constitute a game.

Mass Field Hockey

This game is played as the regular game of field hockey with these exceptions:

1. a large number can play;
2. there is no halftime;
3. all fouls eliminate the persons committing them;
4. after a foul the ball is put in play at the point of the foul between two players of the opposite team;
5. there are no boundary lines, hence the ball is never out of bounds; and
6. 10 minutes constitute a game.

Pin Guard

An Indian club is placed in the center of the playing area. One player is the guard. He has a swatter and stands beside the pin. At a signal, the other players attempt to knock over the pin either by striking it with one hand or kicking it with a foot. The guard attempts to touch any player that comes near him with the swatter. Any player touched by the swatter is temporarily eliminated and withdraws until some player has knocked over the pin. Each time a player is eliminated he scores one dud. Any player knocking over the pin becomes the guard. The old guard joins the attackers. The eliminated players reenter the play at a signal, and the game recommences. The first player to receive three duds must pay a penalty.

Third Degree

The group is divided into two or more teams of 10 to 12 players each, and each team sits in a different corner of the room. Each team selects a representative, and the representatives meet and select some object from any place in the universe to be guessed. The representatives then go to a group other than their own. The group immediately begins to shoot questions at the representative in an effort to find out the name of the object. In answering, the representative may use only *yes, no,* or *I don't know.* Any number of questions may be asked and the object is to guess the mystery object before the other teams do. New representatives are chosen for the next game.

Circle Soccer Tag

This game is played with any number of players who form a circle with one player, IT, inside. The other players may enter the circle with only one foot. The players kick the ball to each other in an attempt to keep IT from getting hit. Players may kick, head butt, or use their bodies on the ball, but may not use their hands. Any player who touches the ball with his hands or who is responsible for IT getting the ball, or who causes IT to go out of bounds for the ball, becomes IT.

Somersault Tag

This game is played as ordinary tag, except that a player being chased by IT may exempt himself from tagging by turning a somersault on the ground. After turning a forward roll a player may sit until he chooses to get up. Once he has risen, however, he is liable to tagging again until he executes another forward roll.

Football Tag

The players are scattered over the playing area. One player is IT and is given a ball. At a signal, IT kicks the ball about, attempting to hit some player with it. Both IT and the players run about where they will in the playing area, but only IT may run out of bounds. IT may dribble the ball as he pleases. Any player touched by the ball becomes IT and takes up the duties of this office at once.

Master of the Ring

A circle is drawn on the ground. The players stand shoulder-to-shoulder inside the circle with arms folded either on the chest or behind the back. The play starts on a signal, and consists of trying to push one's neighbor out of the circle using the shoulders only. Any player overstepping the circle drawn on the ground drops out of the game. Any player who unfolds his arms or falls down is also out of the game. The master of the ring is he who in the end vanquishes all of the others.

Bring Me

The group is divided into teams. Each team chooses a captain. The leader stands across the room and calls for articles that each team member might have on him. Team members help their captain find the article to take to the leader. The first captain who gets the article to the leader gets a point for his team. The leader should ask for about a dozen objects such as a driver's license, lipstick, shoe, class ring, pair of glasses, colored socks, comb, or certain kind of watch. The team with the most points is the winner of the game.

Do This, Do That

The group is arranged in open formation facing front. The leader takes position directly in front of the group where all can see. He calls out loud, "Do this," and at the same moment, executes an exercise-type movement. All of the group must imitate the movement. The leader continues the exercises occasionally saying, "Do that," in place of *do this.* Those players who execute the movement when the leader commands, *do that,* are eliminated and sit down in their positions. The elimination continues until all have been seated. The last player eliminated is the winner.

Soccer Ball Tag

One player is chosen to be the tagger. The other players are scattered inside the playing area. A soccer ball is used. The ball must be played by the feet and may not be controlled by the hands except to protect the face. Players try to secure the ball with their feet and to tag any other player with it. At the same time, they try not to be tagged. Players may not kick the ball into the air higher than the waist of the other players. Each time a player is touched by the ball, no matter how lightly, he becomes the tagger. If a player sees that a ball is going out of bounds he may run outside the playing area and stop it with his feet or hands. If the ball passes out of bounds without being stopped, the nearest person at the point of departure goes after it, returns the ball as rapidly as possible by kicking it or carrying it to the boundary line. He may dribble the ball in himself without losing a point.

Each player starts with five points to his credit. Every time a player is tagged with the ball, he has one point deducted from his score, whenever the kicker sends the ball higher than the waists of the players, one point is deducted for each offense. To use the hands, other than to protect the face, causes the loss of one point for the offending player. When a player's five points are exhausted, he is retired from the game. If he is the kicker when the fifth point is lost, he remains as kicker in the game until he tags another player. As fouls are made, the offending players calls, "One," "Two," or "Three," according to the number of points they had deducted. The player remaining in the game the longest wins.

Nine Court Basketball

The basketball court is divided into nine equal areas. The teams are made up of nine players on each. The game is played as basketball except each player is assigned an area and must stay within that boundary. The players advance the ball toward their goal by passing and they may dribble one time. Only forwards may shoot at the goal. The ball is put into play by a center tossup. An unguarded free throw (worth one point) is awarded for a foul, such as blocking or holding. The ball is taken out of bounds for infractions such as crossing lines and traveling.

Sideline Basketball

This game is played on one half of a regulation basketball court with a basketball. Two members of each team play on the court and players line up on the sidelines, one team on each sideline. Regulation basketball rules are followed, except that the ball may be passed to teammates on the sidelines. Both teams play the same basket. The defensive team becomes offensive by throwing the ball to a player on the sidelines. The center line is out of bounds, and stepping over any line gives the ball to the opposing team on its sideline. The ball may be put into play by a center tossup, or by giving the ball to a player on the sidelines whose team was scored against. The players on the sidelines rotate with players on the floor. Two points are scored for each basket made and one point for a free throw after a foul.

Dens

Each player selects for himself a den: a post, tree, corner of a building, or, if in a gym, a piece of apparatus may serve for this.

One player opens the game by running out from his den, the second player tries to catch (tag) him. The third player may try to catch either of these two, and so on. The object of the different players is to make captives of the other, as any player caught must thereafter join his captor in trying to catch others, thus, eventually aggregating the different players into parties, although each starts separately, and anyone may be the nucleus of a group should he be successful in catching another player. The players may only be caught by those who issue from a den after they themselves have ventured forth. For instance, Number 2 goes out to catch Number 1. Number 3 may catch either Number 2 or 1, but neither of them may catch him. The last player out may catch any of the other players. At any time a player may run back to his den, after which again issuing forth gives him the advantage over all others who may then be out, as he may catch them. As the players are gradually gathered into different parties, the game becomes more concentrated, and the side wins that captures all of the players.

One player may catch only one player at a time.

Prisoner's Base

Two teams are formed and each is assigned to one of the bases which are marked on opposite ends of the play area. Each team has a prisoner near its base. The players try to take all of the opponents as prisoners. A player is taken prisoner when he is tagged by an opponent who left his base after he (the player taken as prisoner) left his. Thus, a player can tag an opponent only if the opponent left his base before he did. Safety is attained by a player who has left his base by capturing an opponent, freeing a prisoner, or returning to his base before he is tagged. A player who has tagged an opponent fairly can take his captive to prison without being tagged. A prisoner can be freed by being tagged by a member of his team who has reached him in prison without being tagged, and both may then return to their base safely. Players may return to their bases at any time, and then they are free to tag any opponent who is out when they leave their base.

Baseball

Equipment: A set of numbered questions written on separate slips of paper. A set of correct answers for the umpire.

Method: Four bases and a pitcher's box are marked out. The group is divided into two sides. The game is played like baseball except that instead of throwing a ball, the pitcher draws a question from a hat and "throws" it to the player at bat. If the batter is unable to answer, he may ask the pitcher the same question. If the pitcher fails, the batter takes a base on balls. If the batter answers correctly, he runs to first. If he does not know the answer and the pitcher does, the batter is out. After a question is thrown the umpire counts to 10. Any member of the opposing team may catch the ball by answering, after the batter has had his chance. Three outs retires the side. Each player returning home scores a run.

Long Ball

Players: 5 to 12 players on each side.

Equipment: Softball and bat.

Playing area: Any outdoor area. Pitcher's box is 30 feet in front of home base. The far base is a three-by-six-foot rectangular area 30 feet beyond the pitcher's box.

Game: The batter hits the ball and runs to the far base. He may stay there or return home. Several players may occupy the far base at one time provided there is a player at bat. When more than one player is on the far base at once, all may return home on a hit. If a base runner leaves the far base, he cannot return unless a fly ball is caught. The batter remains at bat until he hits the ball. Every hit is fair regardless of where the ball lands. A runner is out when (1) a fly ball is caught, (2) the far baseman has the ball before the runner reaches base, or (3) the runner is tagged off base.

Scoring: A run is scored each time a base runner reaches home safely. Three outs constitute a side out. Any number of innings may be played.

Cage Ball

Playing field: 30-by-80 feet, adjusted to age group.

Equipment: Volleyball net and large ball.

Method: The net is eight feet off the floor. Each court is divided into three equal areas starting from the server's back line. Each player can play the area he is in, up to the parallel line. They cannot go back of the line. They may reach over it, but may not step on it. The players rotate to the server's position. The server throws or bats the ball to one of his players who assists it over the net. All served balls must be assisted, or the service goes to the opposing team. Only the serving team scores. When a ball touches the floor or goes into the net or out of bounds, it is a point against the team responsible. The game is 11 points.

Balloon Game

The group is divided into teams. Each member of the team has a balloon. Two chairs are at the head of each team. The object is for each member of the team to race up to the chair, blow up her balloon, sit on it, and break it. The players then run back to their line. The first team to have all their members get finished the quickest are the winners.

E-Mail

Each member of the group chooses a partner and is given a pencil and paper. The players write e-mail messages to their partners using all the letters found in their name (e.g., Theresa = thought he exchanged rings early Sunday afternoon). Then they exchange the messages. The leader may choose to have them read the messages aloud—the funnier the better!

Wink

An uneven number of players are required for this game. Enough chairs are placed in a circle to allow one chair for each two players plus one for the odd player, that is, half as many chairs as there are players, with one player left over. A player sits in each chair, facing inward. Behind each chair stands a second player, who acts as guard. There should be one empty chair with a guard behind it. This odd player winks at someone sitting in the circle, who at once tries to slip out of his chair without being tagged by his guard and take his place in the empty chair. He may not go if he is tagged by his guard. The object of the guards should be to avoid being the keeper of an empty chair, and, therefore, the one who has to wink. The players try to evade the vigilance of the guards by the quickness and unexpectedness of their movements. The guards may not keep their hands on their prisoners, but must have them hanging at their sides until they see their players winked at. They may not dash around the sides of the chairs which they guard, but must stay behind them all the time. Nodding the head may be used instead of winking, but is more apparent to the guard.

Group Fortune Telling

An individual may set up a table or tent and tell the fortune of his "client" using the hand and fingers. The meaning of the various characteristics are listed in the column to the right. It should be emphasized that these characteristics and their messages are for entertainment only and do not imply scientific fact.

Hands:

Are your hands short and square?	Practical
Long and slender?	Artist, great lover, happy disposition
Long and blunt?	Sportsmanlike

Fingers:

Even distance apart?	Very original
Different distances?	Imitative
Bend way back?	Deceitful
Still and strong?	Leadership
Does the end of little finger come above the joint of next finger?	You rule the house
Does the end of little finger come below the joint of next finger?	The house rules you, or tries to

Nails:

Long and white?	Selfish
Red nails?	Bad temper
Spots?	Gift for each spot (poor manicuring)

Life line (around base of thumb):

Clear?	Long healthy life
Vague or broken?	Vice versa
Broken same place in both hands?	Accident

Heart line (across hand close to fingers):

Clear?	Good health, lots of friends
Vague or broken?	Vice versa

Group Fortune Telling

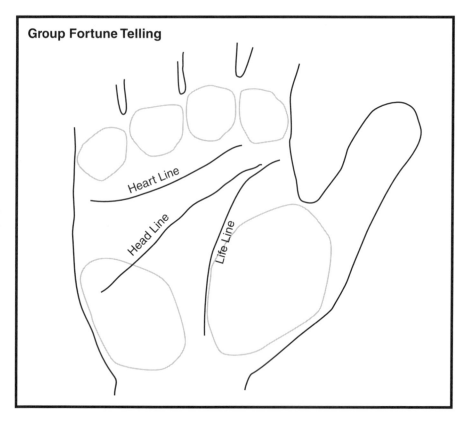

Head line (across hand about center, parallel heart):

Straight across?	Greedy
Turns up?	Misfortune
Turns down?	Excellent character
Divides at end?	Live double life

More Relay Races

All Fours Relay

The teams are divided in half and the halves are arranged in columns facing each other, abreast of two common lines 40 feet apart; teams standing in parallel lines about 10 feet apart. At a signal, the first player in half A of each team runs on all fours toward half B, touching off the first player of that group of the line. This player runs on all fours toward half A, touching off the second player of this group. This continues until all have run. The team that has its last player cross the opposite line first wins.

Worm Relay

The teams are arranged in parallel columns of files, 10 feet apart, abreast of a common line—players standing at normal intervals. The finish line is 50 feet forward and parallel with the starting line. All of the players sit down with knees bent so that their feet are close to the buttocks. Each player reaches back, grasps the ankles of her teammate behind her, and raises her buttocks from the floor and moves forward as a team. The team that completely crosses the finish line first, providing its column is unbroken, wins. Any team breaking its column regroups and begins again (either at the point of the break or at the starting line).

Arch Ball Relay

The teams are arranged in parallel columns of files, 10 feet apart abreast of a common line—players standing so that the chest of each touches the back of the player in front. The first player of each team starts with a ball. All of the players raise their hands overhead. At a signal, the first player in each column passes the ball backward over his head to the second player, who passes it on to the third. The ball is passed in this way to the end of the column. The last player of the column catches the ball, runs with it to the head of the column, steps in front of the column and passes it backward as before. The ball must be touched by each player each time it is passed. This continues until all players have run. The team that arrives in its original position first wins.

Arm Carry Relay

The teams are arranged in parallel columns of files, 10 feet apart, abreast of a common line. The leader establishes a turning point 40 feet in front of each team. The second player in each column stands sideways immediately in front of the first player and places his near arm across the first player's neck. The first player leans forward and placing one arm under the knees and the other arm under the waist picks up the second player. At a signal, the first player in each column, carrying the second player in this manner, runs forward to the turning point. Here the carrier drops the rider to the floor. The first player remains here, the second player runs back to the starting line, picks up the third player as previously outlined, and carries him to the turning point. This continues until all have been carried forward. The team finishing first wins.

Arm Roll Relay

Two teams are arranged in parallel lines 10 feet apart. The players of each team stand shoulder-to-shoulder with arms raised forward and curved so all of the arms together form a trough. The first player of each team starts with a ball. At a signal, the first person in the column rolls the ball in the trough of arms. The other players of the team roll it toward the foot of the line. The last person receives it and carries it to the head of the line and rolls it in the trough toward the foot of the line. After rolling the ball, the player takes a position at the head of the line with his arms held forward. Each player carries the ball forward in turn until all have run. The team arriving at its original formation first wins.

Avalanche Relay

The teams are arranged in parallel columns 10 feet apart abreast of a common line. The finish line is 30 feet in front of and parallel to the starting line. The players of each column are spaced at intervals of eight feet. The last player in each column runs forward to the person directly in front and clasps her about the hips with her hands. The two run forward in this manner to the next player, who is likewise clasped about the waist. The gradually accumulating body moves forward to the first person in the column, and then on to the finish line. The team that wholly crosses the finish line first wins.

Back Carry Relay

The teams are arranged in parallel columns 10 feet apart, abreast of a common line. The first two players of each column stand back-to-back and link elbows. At a signal, the leading player in each column leans forward and, lifting the other player, who raises his feet, carries him forward to the turning point. Here they halt and the carrier lowers the player on his back, without changing their relative positions. This player immediately bends forward, lifting the first player upon his back and runs back to the starting line. At this point, one of them tags the second pair, who have taken the back-to-back position while the first pair was running. The second pair repeats the performance of the first, touching off the next pair at the starting line. This continues until all have run. The team finishing first wins.

Backward Running Relay

The teams are arranged in parallel columns 10 feet apart, abreast of a common line. A turning point is established 50 feet in front of each column. The first player of each column turns around so his back is toward the turning point. At a signal, this player, traveling backwards, runs to, or around, the turning point and back to the starting line. On reaching the starting line he tags the second player, who repeats the action. This continues until all have run. The team finishing first wins.

Ball Throw Relay

Two parallel lines are established 40 to 100 feet apart. The group is divided into two equal teams. The teams are divided in half and each half is arranged in a column, facing each other from opposite baselines. The first player of half A of each team starts with a ball (baseball, basketball, soccer, or playground ball). At a signal, the player with the ball throws it to the first player of half B, who receives it and throws it back to the second player of half A, who returns it to the second player of half B. The ball is thrown back and forth in this manner, each player catching and throwing it in turn until all have handled it. The last player of half B throws it to the first player of A. The ball may only be thrown from in back of the line and caught in back of the line. Any player dropping the ball must recover it himself and throw it. The team placing its ball in its original holder's hands first wins.

Ball Pass and Run Relay

The teams are arranged in parallel lines 10 feet apart, with the players in each line four feet apart. Two distinct turning points are established, one 10 feet to the right of each line of players, and one 10 feet to the left of each line. The player at the right end of each team starts with a ball. At a signal, the player with the ball passes it to the second player, who passes it to the third, and so on down the line to the last player. This player, carrying the ball, runs to the left turning point and then back to the right turning point, running zigzag through the line of players, alternately going behind and in front of each successive player. After touching or rounding the right turning point, the runner passes the ball to the first player in the line and the ball is immediately passed to the end of the line as before. The first runner, after passing the ball, drops in at the right end of the line. This continues, each player moving one place to the left. Each player running with the ball must touch or round both turning points. The team finishing in its original position first wins.

Ball Pass Relay

The teams are arranged in parallel lines 10 feet apart, players in each line standing six feet apart. The first player of each line starts with a ball. At a signal, the player with the ball passes it to the second player. This player passes it to the third, the third passes it to the fourth. The ball is passed in this way, each player catching and passing the ball to the next, to the end of the line and back to the starting point. The team that places the ball in its first player's hand first wins. This game may be varied by having the ball go up and back two, three, or more times; or also by prescribing the method of passing and catching, or, finally, by having multiple balls being passed at the same time.

Ball Roll Relay

The teams are arranged in parallel columns of files, 10 feet apart, abreast of a common line. One player starts with feet spread, 40 feet in front of each column. If a wall is available, the columns should be arranged so these players may be placed abreast of it, five feet from the same. If no wall is available, an extra player may stand just beyond the player standing straddle-legged. A line is drawn half way between the player standing with feet spread and the column. This is the throwing line. The first player of each column starts with a ball. At a signal, the first player runs forward to the throwing line; from here he attempts to roll the ball between the legs of the player in front. If he is not successful, he recovers the ball and tries again from the same throwing line. The thrower has three trials. Upon making a successful throw or completing his third attempt, he returns the ball to the second player in the column, who repeats this performance. The player standing forward with feet spread neither aids nor interferes with the throwers. The only duty of the player beyond the one standing straddle-legged is to recover the ball and return it to the thrower. This continues until all have competed. The team having its last player across the starting line with the ball first wins.

Basketball Point Relay

The teams are arranged in parallel lines 10 feet apart, the first player of each team being abreast of a common line which should run parallel to a basketball hoop and about 20 feet from it. All of the players spread their legs. The first player of each team starts with a basketball. At a signal, the player with the ball rolls the ball back between the spread legs of his teammates. The last player catches the ball, runs forward, and tries to put the ball through the hoop. Succeeding or failing he recovers the ball, runs with it to the head of the column, and rolls it back between the legs of his teammates. This continues until all have made a try at the basket. Each successful throw counts one point for the team. The team making the most points wins.

Basket Shooting Relay

A basketball hoop is required for this game. The teams are arranged in parallel columns 10 feet apart, abreast of a common line; this line is drawn parallel to and 20 feet from a basketball hoop. A turning point is established 10 feet in back of each team. The players spread their feet and the first player in each column starts with a ball. At a signal, he rolls the ball back between his legs and the legs of his teammates. The other players of the team, if necessary, assist in rolling the ball back. The last player in the column picks up the ball, runs back to, or around, the turning point, and then runs forward and shoots the basket in front. Each runner has five trials at shooting the basket. Upon making a basket, or at the end of the fifth trial, the player returns with the ball to the front of the column and rolls it backward between the spread legs. The last player, upon returning with the ball to the front of the column and throwing it back, drops in at the front of the column. This continues until all have run forward. The team completing its task first wins.

Blind Man Relay

The teams are arranged in a single columns of files, 10 feet apart, abreast of a common line. A stone or a ball is placed directly in front of each team on the starting line and another is placed 40 feet in front of each team. The players of each team are divided into pairs and the first pair of each team starts with a towel. At a signal, the player with the towel wraps it around his partner's eyes, tying it behind his head. As soon as the blindfold is adjusted, both players run forward. The player with eyes unbound directs his partner to the opposite stone, which he must touch. All directing should be by word of mouth and not by bodily contact. As soon as he touches the stone, the towel is removed and wrapped about the eyes of the other player who is then directed back to the stone at the starting line. After the stone has been touched, the towel is taken off and passed to the second pair who repeat the performance of the first pair. The team that first has its final pair touch the stone at the starting line wins.

Bounce and Pass Relay

The teams are arranged in parallel columns of files, 10 feet apart, abreast of a common line, the players in each column four feet apart. The first player in each column starts with a ball. At a signal, the player with the ball bounces it on the floor, and throws it back over his head to the second player. The second player and all players behind him repeat. The last player, upon receiving the ball, runs forward to the front of the column, steps four feet in front of the leading player, bounces the ball on the floor, and passes it back over his head. This continues until all have run forward. The team finishing in its original position first wins.

Bounce Between Legs Relay

The teams are arranged in parallel columns of files, 10 feet apart, players standing four feet apart with feet spread. The first player of each team starts with a ball. At a signal, the player with the ball bounces it backward between his legs so the second player can catch it. The second player catches it and the ball is bounced backward in this fashion to the last player. When the last player has it, all of the players turn around and bounce it, in the same way back to the first player. Any player dropping the ball must recover it, return to his position in the column and pass it in the required manner to the next player. The team returning the ball to the head of its column first wins. The game may be varied by having the ball make two, three, or four trips.

Bounding the Waves Relay

The teams are arranged in double columns 10 feet apart, abreast of a common line. The players of each team face inward and grasp hands with their teammates, thus forming a trough of hands. The first two players of each column release hands. One of these players jumps into the trough of hands. Here he lies stiffly on his back, arms by his sides, and head up the trough. He is passed up to the other end of the trough, and when the last two players help him get off, he immediately runs around the head of the lines, touches the next player (the player who formerly held hands with him), and then returns to the foot, where he takes position. The second player jumps into the trough as soon as he is touched. He is passed to the foot, is placed on the ground, and continues as the first player did. After touching the third player at the front, he returns to the foot, where he joins hands with his former partner. This continues until all have gone through the trough. The team that finishes first with its players in their original position wins.

Brick Walk Relay

The teams are divided in half and the halves are arranged in columns facing each other, abreast of two common lines, 20 feet apart. Two bricks, or flat boards as large as bricks, are placed on the line in front of the half of each team. At a signal, the first player of half A of each team steps on the two bricks. Bending forward, he stands on one brick, grasps the other and places it forward, steps onto it, grasps the other, places it forward, steps onto it, and continues to the opposite line. When he has placed both bricks on the opposite line, he steps off them. The first player of half B steps onto them in the same manner and proceeds to half A's line. Here the second player of half A steps onto them and proceeds across. This continues until all have run. The team that has its last player across the opposite line first wins.

Caterpillar Relay

The teams are arranged in parallel columns of files, 10 feet apart, abreast of a common line. A turning point is established 60 feet in front of each team. The first two players of each team start with a six-foot-long stick. The first two players of each team face each other and get astride of the stick, holding the same with both hands, one hand in front and the other hand in back. At a signal, the pair with the stick run to the turning point, one traveling forward and one backward. On reaching the turning point they stop, and without turning, run back to the starting line. They are now running reversed. On reaching the starting line, they drop the stick. The second pair pick it up, adjust it between their legs, and continue as the first. The third pair follows and so forth. This continues until all have run. The team that first has its last pair of players across the starting line wins.

Centipede Relay

The teams are arranged in parallel columns of files, 10 feet apart, abreast of a common line. A turning point is established 60 feet in front of each column. The first two players of each team start with a stick and place it between their legs, holding it with one hand. At a signal, the pair holding the stick run forward to, or around, the turning point and return to the starting line, where they drop the stick. The next two players pick up the stick, adjust it in the same way, and proceed. This continues, each successive pair of players running together until all have run. The team that has its last pair across the starting line first wins. This race may be varied by having a larger number of players carry the stick.

Chain Relay

The teams are arranged in parallel columns of files, 10 feet apart, abreast of a common line. A turning point is established 40 feet in front of each column. The players compete in pairs. The rear player of the first pair reaches down and takes hold of the ankles of the person in front. The leading person puts his hands on the ground. At a signal, this pair, keeping this position, runs forward to, or around, the turning point. Here they exchange positions and then return to the starting line. At the starting line, the leader touches off the first player of the next pair who have taken the traveling position at the starting line as the first pair did. Successive groups repeat until all have run. The team having its last pair across the starting line first wins.

Chariot Relay

The teams are arranged in parallel columns of four, abreast of a common line, and standing 10 feet apart. A turning point is established 80 feet in front of each team. The first group of four players of each team starts with a six-foot-long stick. These players, using both hands, hold the stick across the front of their chests. At a signal, the quartet with the stick runs forward to, or around, the turning point and tries to return to the starting line before a similar quartet from the other team can. At the starting line, the first group passes the stick to the second group, who repeat the run. This continues until all have run. The team that has its last group across the starting line first wins. The race may also be carried out by having each set of players link arms, hold hands, or place their arms about each other's shoulders.

Circle Cap Relay

A circle 15 feet in diameter is drawn on the playing area. The teams are arranged in columns at regular intervals about the circle, each column starting at the circle and projecting outward—players facing in (see illustration). The first player of each group starts with a baton. At a signal, the first player of each team runs to the right around the circle. Arriving at his starting position, he hands the baton to the second player who continues about the circle. Each runner, upon finishing, makes for his original position. All runners, after the first, run through their gaps so as not to interfere with other runners. Any player who is tagged by the player behind is eliminated, thereby also eliminating his team. Players who are tagged withdraw from the circle. The other players may run through these positions until the relay is finished. The race continues until all have run. The team finishing first or remaining in the race after all of the others have been eliminated wins.

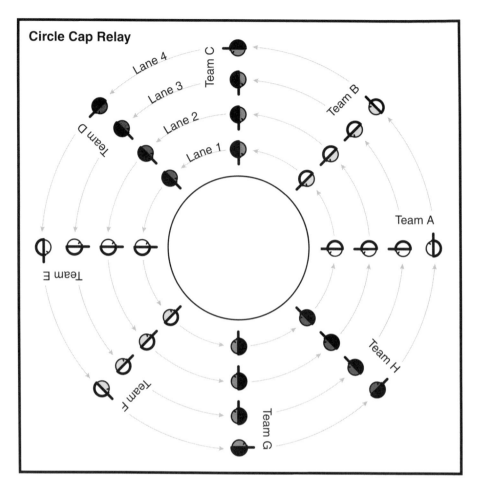

Circle Cap Relay

Crab Walk Relay

The teams are arranged in parallel columns of files, 10 feet apart, abreast of a common line. A turning point is established 50 feet in front of each team. The first player in each column sits on the ground, feet in front, hands in back. At a signal, he raises his body from the ground, and traveling in this position, walks forward to, or around, the turning point and returns to the starting line. As soon as the first player leaves the starting line, the second player takes the same position and starts forward, following the track of the first. The other players follow in succession. They must follow in column. The team that has its last player across the starting line first wins.

Crawl and Run Relay

The teams are arranged in parallel columns of files, 10 feet apart, abreast of a common line, players standing at normal intervals with feet spread. At a signal, the last player in each column drops onto his hands and knees and crawls forward between the legs of the other players in the column. On arriving at the front of the column, he rises and runs to the rear of the column, where he touches the next player. He then falls in, in his regular position. The player touched drops on his hands and knees and crawls forward between the legs of those in front, rises and runs around to the last player, drops down and crawls under his legs and rises to touch the next player, and then falls in, in his regular position. The race continues in this manner, each player in turn crawling through the legs of the players in front, running to the rear of the column, and crawling forward to his starting position in the column throughout the relay and not running ahead of slow players in front. The team finishing in its original place first wins.

Crooked Man Relay

The teams are arranged in parallel columns of files, 10 feet apart, abreast of a common line. A turning point is established 10 feet in front of each team. At a signal, the first player of each team travels forward to the winning line, advancing in the following manner: rocking forward onto the left toe and stepping the right toe across in back of the left; rocking forward onto the right toe and stepping the left foot across in back of the right, and so on, attempting to advance two or three inches each step. At the turning point, the contestant turns and runs back to the starting line, touching off the second player. The second player and the others repeat his performance until all have competed. The team finishing first wins.

Crawl Through Legs Relay

The teams are arranged in parallel columns of files, 10 feet apart, abreast of a common line. At a signal, the first player steps forward and spreads his feet. Immediately the second player crawls through the first player's legs and rises close in front of him with feet spread. The third player in the column crawls through the legs of the first two, coming up in front of the second player. The others follow in succession. As the players come up from between the legs and stand in a closed column, each holds the player in front about the waist. The team that has its last player standing in front first wins.

Dead Man Relay

The teams are arranged in parallel columns of files, 10 feet apart, abreast of a common line, players standing with feet spread. A turning point is established 30 feet in front of each column. One player lies face down on the turning point, body stiff and head toward the column. At a signal, the first player of each team runs forward to the turning point, places his hands under the shoulders of the player lying there, and lifts him to the standing position. The lifter immediately lies down into the place vacated by the player he lifted. The player lifted runs back to the rear of his column. As the runner passes the column, each player puts his right hand back between his legs. The runner taps the right hand of the last player. The last player tags the player in front of him, this player tags the player in front, and so on, until the first player is tagged. This player runs forward and repeats the performance of the first player. All tagging should be by the right hand on the right hand. This continues until all have run forward. The team arriving in its original position first wins.

Dizzy Walk Relay

The teams are arranged in parallel columns of files, 10 feet apart, abreast of a common line. A turning point is established 40 feet in front of each column. The first player in each column starts with a short stick three-feet long. At a signal, this player puts his hand on top of the stick, places his head on his hands, and runs around the stick four times and then, dropping the stick, walks toward the turning point. At the turning point, he executes a backward roll and then runs back to the starting line, where he picks up the stick and hands it to the second player who repeats. The third, fourth, and other players repeat until all have completed the course. The team that has its last player across the starting line first wins.

Double Hopping Relay

The teams are arranged in parallel columns of twos, 10 feet apart, abreast of a common line. A turning point is established 60 feet in front of each column. Each player places his inside arm about the shoulders of his partner and together hop as one to the turning point and back. At a signal, the first pair touches a member of the second pair, who immediately repeat the performance of the first pair. This continues until all have run. The team finishing first wins.

Donkey Relay

The teams are arranged in parallel columns of files, 10 feet apart, abreast of a common line. A turning point is established 50 feet in front of each team. At a signal, Player 2 in each column leaps on Player 1's back. Player 1, carrying Player 2 in this manner, runs forward to the turning point, where he drops his burden. Player 1 remains behind at the turning point. Player 2 runs back and carries Player 3 up to the turning point and drops him. Player 3 returns for Player 4. This continues until all have been carried forward. The team that has its last player reach the turning point first wins.

Note:
The player who rides down runs back and carries the next player down.

Double Jumping Relay

The playing area is a small circular track 50 yards in circumference. The teams competing in the race are spaced at regular intervals about the track. The first player of each team starts with a belt. At a signal, the player with the belt wraps it about his ankles. Tying his two feet tightly together, and then starts jumping around the track. After making a circuit of the track, the jumper unwraps the belt and passes it to the next member of his team, who repeats. He passes it to the next, and so forth. This continues until all have competed. The team finishing first wins.

Double Roll Relay

This relay should be executed on mats or in grass. The players are arranged in parallel columns of files, 10 feet apart, abreast of a common line. A turning point is established 30 feet in front of each column. Player 1 of each team lies on his back, feet toward the turning point, and raises his legs vertically. Player 2 stands one foot on each side of the first player's head and grasps the ankles of Player 1. Player 1 likewise grasps the ankles of Player 2. At a signal, the players, maintaining their grasp, roll forward, each executing forward rolls over and under the other. When they have crossed the turning point, both release their grasp. Player 1 remains behind, Player 2 runs back for and positions himself as Player 1 did, Player 3 positioning himself as Player 2 did and both roll forward. At the turning line, they disengage as before, Player 2 remains and Player 3 runs back for Player 4. This continues until all have reached the turning line. The team having all of its players across the turning point first wins.

Double Rope Skip Relay

The teams are arranged in parallel columns of twos, 10 feet apart, abreast of a common line. A turning point is established 60 feet in front of each column. The first pair of players in each column starts with a 10-foot-long rope. Each player holds one end of the rope in his outside hand and links his inside elbow with his partner. At a signal, the first pair runs forward to, or around, the turning point and returns to the starting line, skipping the rope all the way. At the starting line, they pass the rope to the second pair, who repeat the performance. In any case, where skipping is halted, the players must halt their forward progress until skipping has been resumed. In other words, there must be no progress without skipping. Each pair runs in turn until all have run. The team having its last pair across the starting line first wins.

Down and up Relay

The teams are arranged in parallel columns of files, 10 feet apart, abreast of a common line. The players in each column stand three feet apart. All the players on each team spread their legs and lean forward. At a signal, the first player in the column passes an object back between her legs to the next player, who passes it on in the same way. When the last player in the column gets the object, he shouts, "Down." On this command, the other players of the team crouch to the ground. The last player with legs astraddle, runs forward over the other players, who have huddled close to the ground. When he reaches the front of the column, all rise and the object is passed back between the legs as before. The last player carries it forward as before. Upon arriving at the front of the column, each player takes up position there. This continues until all have run forward. The team returning to its original position first wins.

Dribble Ball Relay

The teams are arranged in parallel lines 10 feet apart, the players on each team six feet apart. The first player of each team starts with a ball that will bounce. At a signal, the first player turns around once and bounces it to the second. The ball should be thrown so that one bounce will put it into the hands of the next player. The second player, after receiving the ball, turns around once and bounces it to the third. The ball is in this way bounced to the end of the line and back to the starting point. The team returning the ball to its first player first wins.

Dumbbell Rush Relay

The teams are arranged in parallel columns 10 feet apart, abreast of a common line. A dumbbell is placed on the ground before the first player of each column. The first player in each column starts with a short stick. At a signal, this player, using only the stick, pushes the dumbbell forward to, or around, a given point and returns. As the bell recrosses the starting line, the first player passes the stick to the second player, who makes the run and passes it to the third player and so on, until all have run. The dumbbell must be pushed and not flung. Any player who fails to comply with this rule, eliminates his team. The team that has its last player across the starting line first wins.

Elbow Swing Relay

The teams are arranged in parallel columns, 10 feet apart, abreast of a common line. The players in each column stand at intervals of eight or ten feet. The starting line is 10 feet in front of each column and the finishing line is 10 feet in back of each column. A player from each team stands at the starting line, each directly in front of his column. At a signal, he runs to the first person in his column. The two players link right elbows, circle about once and release. The player who started falls into the first player's position. The first player links elbows with the second. Both swing around once and release. The first player falls into the second player's position, and the second player links elbows with the third. This continues until all have circled around. The last player runs to the finish line. The team finishing first wins.

Elephant Walk Relay

The teams are arranged in parallel columns of files, 10 feet apart, abreast of a common line. A turning point is established 40 feet in front of each team. At a signal, the first player of each team stands with his hands and feet on the floor and, with elbows and knees rigid, runs forward to, or around, the turning point and back to the starting line. Here, he touches off the second player who repeats. This continues until all have run. The team finishing first wins.

Gap Bowl Relay

The teams are arranged in parallel columns of files, 10 feet apart, abreast of a common line. A line three-feet long is established 30 feet in front of each column—this is the bowling line (see illustration). Two Indian clubs are placed three feet apart, halfway between, and parallel to the starting line and the bowling line—one pair of clubs for each team. The first player of each team starts with a ball. At a signal, the first player runs forward to the bowling line, and standing behind the line, he attempts to roll the ball between the clubs. If the ball rolls to one side, the second player at the line returns the ball to him. If he knocks over a club, he must run and set up the club. The other player returns the ball to him as before. If he succeeds, the second player picks up the ball, runs forward and makes the attempt. Each player in turn runs forward and bowls until all have competed. The first player serves as assistant to the last. The team finishing first wins.

Engine and Tender Relay

The teams are arranged in columns 10 feet apart, abreast of a common line. The second player (the tender) of each column starts with a flat object, such as a book, slipper, or block of wood. At a signal, the tender places the object on the first player's head. The first player (the engine) runs to the right around the rear of the column and back to his position. Here, the third player (the next tender) removes the object from the engine's head and places it on the first tender's head making him an engine. The second engine runs forward around the first player, back around the last, and returns to his position. Here, the fourth player removes the object and places it on the third player's head. This

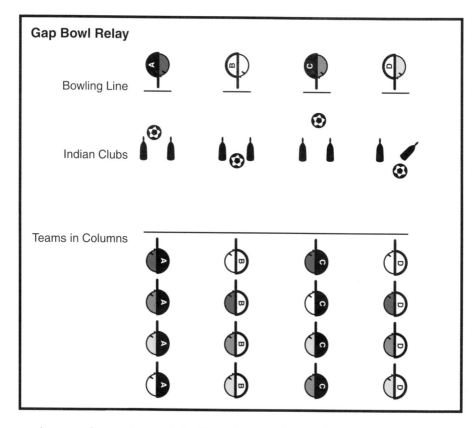

Gap Bowl Relay
Bowling Line
Indian Clubs
Teams in Columns

engine runs forward around the first player and second player, back around the last player, and returns to his position, where the relay continues as before. The engine must never touch the object with his hands. If the block drops off the head of any engine, he must stop at the point where it falls and wait until the tender puts it back. The tender is not allowed to touch it until it hits the floor. The players of each column must remain at normal intervals. The team finishing first wins.

Additional Comments:
- This game should not be played when there is a possibility of any children in the group having head lice.

Feet and Club Relay

The teams are arranged in parallel column of files, 10 feet apart and abreast of a common line. An Indian club is placed, standing on end, 30 feet in front of each column. At a signal, the first player of each team runs forward to the club, sits on the ground, kicks over the club, and sets it up again, using only his feet. When the club is set up again, he rises and returns to the starting line, where he touches off the second player. The second player repeats the performance of the first. This continues until all have run. The team that has its last player across the starting line first wins.

Floor Dribble Relay

The teams are arranged in columns, 10 feet apart, and abreast of a common line. The first player of each column starts with a ball that will bounce. At a signal, the player with the ball rolls it backward between his legs. Other players in the column, as needed, help roll it along to the end of the column. The last player picks it up and using a regular basketball dribble, dribbles to the front of the column. Here he catches the ball, steps in front of the column, and rolls it back between the legs of his teammates, who, as before, help it along, if necessary. If at any time the ball rolls outside of the legs of the players, it must be recovered and started again from the point of its exit. Each player, in his turn, dribbles the ball forward and after passing the ball back remains in front of the column. The team arriving at its original position first wins.

Foot Dribble Relay

The teams are arranged in parallel columns 10 feet apart, abreast of a common line. The players in each column are spaced eight feet apart. The finishing line is 30 feet in front of the columns. At a signal, the last player in each column does a forward roll and coming to his feet, touches the player in front of him. This player repeats the roll and touches the player in front of him. This continues until all have rolled. The player at the head of the column, after executing his roll, runs forward to the finishing line. The team that has its leading player cross the finishing line first wins.

Gallop Relay

The teams are arranged in parallel columns of files, 10 feet apart, abreast of a common line. A turning point is established 60 feet in front of each team. At a signal, the first player of each team puts one foot forward and then gallops to, or around, the turning point and back to the starting line. The foot placed forward at the beginning must be kept forward throughout the run. At the starting line, the first player touches off the second player, who repeats. This continues until all have competed. The team finishing first wins.

Goat Relay

The teams are arranged in parallel columns of files, 10 feet apart, abreast of a common line. The first player of each team starts with a ball. At a signal, this player rolls the ball back between his legs. Each player in the column, as needed, helps move the ball toward the rear of the column. The last player (the goat) stops the ball, and walking on all fours, bumps it with his head to the front of the column. The ball should not be touched by the goat's hands in its forward progress. Then, using his hands, the goat rolls the ball between the legs of the players in the column. The ball should never be lifted off the floor. After delivering the ball the goat falls in at the front of the column. The last player in the column receives the ball and proceeds as his predecessor did. This continues until all have run forward. The team finishing first wins.

Head Balance Relay

The teams are arranged in parallel columns of files, 10 feet apart, abreast of a common line. A turning point is established 30 feet in front of each column. The first player of each column starts with a flat object such as a book, beanbag, or a sneaker. All should be given the same kind of an object. At a signal, the player with the object balances it on his head and walks or runs forward to, or around, the given point and back to the starting line. At the starting line the second player takes the object off the first player's head, puts it on his own, and repeats. Players must carry their arms at their sides and not touch the object with their hands while advancing, unless it falls and hits the floor. Any player dropping the object from his head must stop on the spot and balance it on his head before he continues. The race continues until all have run. The team having its last runner cross the starting line first wins.

Additional Comments:
  • This game should not be played when there is a possibility of any children in the group having head lice.

Heel Run Relay

The teams are arranged in parallel columns of files, 10 feet apart, abreast of a common line. A turning point is established 40 feet in front of each team. At a signal, the first player of each team, traveling on his heels, runs forward to, or around, the turning point and back to the starting line, where he touches the second player. The second player repeats the performance of the first. The third, fourth, and others repeat until all have run. The team finishing first wins.

Hop Step Relay

The teams are arranged in parallel columns of files, 10 feet apart, and abreast of a common line. A turning point is established 60 feet in front of each team. At a signal, the first player of each team, advancing by alternately hopping and stepping, travels to, or around, the turning point and back to the starting line.

For example, the player advances as follows: step onto left foot, hop on left foot, step onto right foot, hop on right foot, step onto left foot, and so on. Steps and hops may be made as long as desired. At the starting line the first player touches off the second who repeats. This continues until all have competed. The team finishing first wins.

Note:
This is not a gallop—the hop is made as long as the players can make it.

Hopping Relay

Each team is divided in half. Each half is arranged in columns facing each other, abreast of two common lines, 60 feet apart. The teams should be 10 feet apart. At a signal, the first player in half A of each column hops on one foot to the starting line of half B. At this point he touches off the first player in half B. This player, hopping on one foot, returns to half A, where he touches off the second player. This hopping back and forth continues until all have competed. The team that has its last player cross the opposite line first wins.

Human Wheelbarrow Relay

The teams are arranged in parallel columns of files, 10 feet apart, abreast of a common line. A turning point is established 30 feet in front of each column. At a signal, the first player of each column puts his hands on the ground. The second grasps the first player's ankles and lifts his feet off the ground. Retaining this position, they advance to or beyond the turning point, here they change positions, the second player walking on his hands and the first player carrying the second player's feet. They then return to the starting point. As the first two players cross the starting line the next two take positions as described as the first two and start forward. This continues until all have run. The team that has its last pair of players cross the finish line first wins.

Indian File Relay

The teams are arranged in parallel columns, 10 feet apart, abreast of a common line. Each team is divided into two, three, or four equal parts. The members of each section place their arms about the waists, on the hips, or on the shoulders of the players in front. At a signal, the first section runs forward to, or around, the turning point, and returns to the starting point, where the leader of the first section touches off the leader of the second section. The second section repeats the performance of the first. This continues until all have run. Sections that break as they run must reunite at once or be disqualified. The team that has its last section cross the starting line first wins.

Juggle Relay

The teams are arranged in parallel columns of files, 10 feet apart, and abreast of a common line, players standing three feet apart with legs spread. The last player of each column starts with a ball. At a signal, the player rolls the ball forward between the legs of his teammates, who as needed, help the ball on its course. The first player picks it up and, repeatedly batting it in the air, juggles it to the back of the column. Here he catches it, steps in back of the column and rolls it forward between the legs of his team, who help it along to the front. If at any time, the ball escapes the path of the legs, it must be secured and started again from the path of its exit. Each player in his turn runs back juggling the ball, and after passing it forward, takes a position in the back of the column. The team arriving at its original position first wins the game.

Jump Stick Relay

The teams are arranged in parallel columns of files, 10 feet apart, abreast of a common line. A turning point is established 20 feet in front of each column and another is established 20 feet in back of each column. The first player in each column starts with a stick six-feet long. At a signal, the first player runs forward with the stick, touches the turning point and returns, handing one end of the stick to the second player, who has stepped off to the side. These two players, one on each side of the column, run back to the end of the column, carrying the stick close to the ground. Each player in the column jumps over the stick as it comes to him. After the last player in the column has jumped over the stick, the first player lets go of the stick and falls in at the end of the column. The second player carries the stick to the rear turning point, forward to the forward turning point, returns to the front of the column, and hands one end to the third player. These two players carry the stick back along the column as previously described. This is continued until all the players have carried the stick forward. The team arriving in its original position first wins.

Kangaroo Relay

The teams are arranged in parallel columns of files, 10 feet apart, abreast of a common line. A turning point is established 25 feet in front of each column. The first player of each column starts with a ball which he places between his ankles, holding it off the ground. At a signal, holding the ball in this position, the first player jumps to, or around, the turning point and returns to the starting line. Upon reaching the starting line, the player drops the ball, the second player picks it up, puts it between his ankles, and proceeds forward. If a ball falls from a player, he must halt and replace the ball at the point of the fall. The team that has the last player return across the starting line first wins.

Lame Chicken Relay

The players are arranged in parallel columns of files, 10 feet apart, abreast of a common line. Ten objects (e.g., stones, beanbags, or dumbbells) are placed in a line two feet apart directly in front of each team. At a signal, the first player of each team, hopping over one object at a time, advances to the far end of the line of objects. Here, the player kicks the last object out of position, replaces it, and then hops over one object at a time to return to the starting place. At the starting point, he touches off the second player, who repeats this performance. This continues until all have taken part. Players must hop on one foot. Any player touching any object but the last, touching his uplifted foot to the floor, jumping over more than one object at a time, or failing to jump over an object, must return to the starting line and start over. The team having its last player over the finishing line first is the winner.

Lame Dog Relay

The players are arranged in parallel columns of files, 10 feet apart, abreast of a common line. A turning point is established 50 feet in front of each team. The first player of each column supports himself on both hands and one foot, the other foot is held out backward. At a signal, retaining this position, he travels to, or around, the turning point and back to the starting line. At this point, he tags off the second player, who repeats. The uplifted foot should be kept off the floor throughout the race. The others follow until all have run. The team finishing first wins.

Lame Duck Relay

The teams are arranged in parallel files, 10 feet apart, abreast of a common starting line. At a signal, the first player in each column raises one foot forward, grasps it with both hands and hops forward to, or around, the turning point and back to the starting line. He touches off the second player, who repeats. This continues until all have competed. The team finishing first wins.

Low Bridge Relay

The teams are arranged in parallel columns of files, 10 feet apart, abreast of a common starting line. Two players face each other, 10 feet in front of each column. These two players hold a stick three to six feet in length from four to five feet above the ground, depending on the size of the players. The stick should be held at right angles to the column of players. At a signal, the columns move forward, each player going under the stick without touching it. The stick should be held firmly. Each player passes under the stick by leaning backward. Players may not stoop forward. The knees may be bent, but the hands must stay on the hips. Only one player at a time may go. Upon passing under the stick, the player runs around to his right to the rear of the column. The team arriving at its original position first wins.

Leapfrog Relay

The teams are arranged in parallel columns 10 feet apart. The players spread their feet and bend forward, placing their hands on their knees. Players stand as firmly as possible. At a signal, starting with the last player in each column, that player straddle-vaults the players in front of him. When coming to the end of the line, he runs around to the right, back to his starting position. The second player then repeats, and so on, until all players are in original positions. The team returning to the starting position and squatting first wins.

Lift Relay

The teams are arranged in columns 10 feet apart, abreast of a common starting line; the players in each column standing at 10 foot intervals. All of the players lie on their backs and fold their arms on their chests. There should be a distance of four feet separating the head and feet of the players. At a signal, the last player rises to his feet, steps forward, and, placing his hands under the shoulders of the person in front, lifts him to his feet. The second person, on reaching his feet, steps forward and lifts the third person. While being lifted, a player should not in any way assist his lifter. Arms should be kept folded, and knees and hips kept still until the upright position has been reached. The team first getting all its players in the upright position wins.

Measuring Feet Relay

The teams are arranged in parallel columns of files, 10 feet apart, abreast of a common line. A turning point is established 20 feet in front of each team. At a signal, the first player of each team walks forward to the turning line by putting each foot down immediately in front of the other. The heel of the advancing foot should touch the toe of the other. Arriving at the turning point, he turns and runs back to the starting line touching off the second player, who repeats the performance. The others follow in order until all have competed. The team finishing first wins.

Obstacle Relay

The teams are arranged in two columns of parallel files 10 feet apart, abreast of a common starting line. Obstacles of all kinds (e.g., things to crawl under, jump over, climb through, run around, and vault over) are placed in front of each team. Each team must have the same obstacles arranged in the same way.

The leader should demonstrate how each obstacle should be traversed. At a signal, the first player in each column starts, makes a circuit and returns to the starting line, where he touches the second player. The second player then repeats and so forth, until all the players have run. The team that has its last player cross the starting line first is the winner.

One-Handed Ball Relay

The teams are arranged in lines 10 feet apart, players four feet apart. All the players place their left hands behind their backs. The first player of each team starts with a basketball. He holds it in his right hand. At a signal, he passes it to the next player who passes it to the next, and so on until the last player receives it. Each player catches and passes with the right hand only. The last person, on receiving the ball, balances it in his hand and runs to the head of the line and passes the ball to the next player, and then on to the next and so on. Any player dropping the ball must recover it using the right hand only. Runners are not allowed to hold the ball against their bodies. They must balance it freely on one hand. This continues until all have carried the ball forward. The team that arrives at its original position first wins.

Over the Top Relay

The teams are arranged in columns 10 feet apart, abreast of a common starting line. Two players, holding a stick from three to six-feet long, stand 30 feet in front of each column. These players hold the stick as high as they can, at right angles to the columns. The first player in each column starts with a ball. At a signal, the player holding the ball runs forward, tosses the ball over the stick, runs under the stick, catches the ball, and then runs back to the second player, who repeats. This continues until all have run. The team finishing first is the winner.

Overhead Pass Relay

The teams are arranged in parallel columns 10 feet apart, abreast of a common starting line, the players in each column four feet apart. The first player in each column starts with a basketball. At a signal, the ball is passed back, overhead, to the player in back, and then on to the next, to the end of the line. When the last player receives the ball, he passes it overhead to the player in front of him and so on back to the head of the line. Any player dropping the ball must recover it, return to his position, and then continue the pass. The team returning the ball to the leading player first wins the race.

Steeplechase Relay

The teams are arranged in parallel columns of files, 10 feet apart, abreast of a common line, the players in each column five feet apart. A turning point is established 20 feet in front of each line, and another is established 20 feet behind each line. The first player of each team starts with a stick six-feet long. At a signal, the first player runs forward with the stick, touches the turning point, and then returns and hands one end of the stick to the second player, who has stepped off to one side of the line. These two players run toward the end of the column, one on each side of the column. While doing this, they hold the stick so the first player jumps over it, then raise it so that it passes over the second player's head, then lower it for the third to jump over, and so on, to the end of the column. Here, the first player releases the stick and takes position at the end of the line. The second player carries the stick to the rear turning point, forward to the front turning point, and then returns to the front of the line and hands the end to the third player. These two then carry the stick along the line as previously described. This continues until all have carried the stick forward. The team at its original position first wins.

Pass and Catch Relay

The teams are arranged in parallel columns of twos, 10 feet apart, abreast of a common line. A turning point is established 50 feet in front of each line. One of the first players of each column starts with a ball. At a signal, the first pair of players runs to, or around, the turning point, and then back to the starting line. They pass the ball back and forth all the while they are running, no player taking more than one step with the ball in his hand. At the starting line, the ball is handed to one of the players of the second pair. This pair repeats. This continues until all have run. Any player dropping the ball must recover it himself. The team finishing first wins, or the number of times the ball is dropped may be counted, and the team with the fewest drops is the winner.

Pass and Squat Relay

The team is arranged in parallel columns of files, 10 feet apart, abreast of a common starting line. The first player (the base player) stands five feet in front of his column. The base player of each team starts with a basketball or soccer ball. At a signal, the base player passes the ball to the first player in his line. This player catches the ball and passes it back to the base player. Immediately after passing the ball the first player squats. The base player then passes to the second player, who catches it and passes it back to the base and then squats. This continues until all the players have caught the ball and sent it back to the base. Any player dropping the ball must recover it and return to his position before passing it again. The team finishing first wins. Passes can be made in any manner.

Wounded Man Relay

All members of each team are arranged in parallel columns of files, 10 feet apart. The players spread their feet and sit on the ground, sitting so close that each player sits between the legs of the player behind him. After getting in this position, each player lies back, resting on the player in back. All players raise hands to a vertical position. At a signal, the first player of each line rises, sits on the hands of the player next in line, and proceeds to lie down on his back on the hands of his teammates. These players then pass the "wounded man" toward the foot of the column. As soon as the first player is out of the way, the second player follows him. As the players reach the foot of the line, each immediately assumes the lying position. The team that arrives at its original position first wins the race.

Pass Over Relay

The teams are arranged in parallel columns of files, 10 feet apart, abreast of a common line. The first player of each column starts with a basketball. At a signal, the player of each team with the ball steps to the right side of his team and runs toward the foot of his column. At the same time, the second player steps to the left and runs to the foot of the column. The two players pass the ball back and forth over the heads of their teammates. No player may take more than one step while holding the ball. At the foot of the column, the first player drops in behind the last player, and the second player rounds the foot of the column down the right side back to the front, where he hands the ball to the third player, who has already stepped out to the left. This player now runs to the foot with the second player who turns around and runs back up the right side. They pass the ball back and forth all the way. At the foot, the second player falls to the rear and the third player rounds the end and runs down the right side. This continues, until all have returned to the starting order. The team finishing first wins.

Pass Through Hoop Relay

The teams are arranged in parallel columns 10 feet apart, the players of each column standing three feet apart. The first player in each row starts with a hoop three feet in diameter. At a signal, the player passes the hoop over his body (head or feet first, at his option). Upon completing this, he hands the hoop to the second player, who passes it over his body and hands it to the third player. This continues until all have passed the hoop over their bodies. The team finishing first wins.

Paul Revere Relay

The teams are arranged in parallel columns of files, 10 feet apart, abreast of a common line, players standing 10 feet apart. The finish line is 20 feet in front of the columns. A light player from each team is chosen to act as rider. The rider starts at the rear of his column. At a signal, the rider mounts the hips of the last person, who carries him forward to the player immediately in front of him. Here, the rider transfers to the back of the second person. The transfer must take place without the rider touching the ground. The second player carries him to the third and so on. The player at the head of the column carries the rider to the finish line. The team carrying its rider across the finish line first wins.

Place Rope Skip Relay

The teams are arranged in parallel lines 10 feet apart, players five feet apart. The first player of each team starts with a rope eight-feet long. At a signal, the player with the rope skips in place 15 times, any style. Upon completing his fifteenth skip he hands the rope to the second player in line. This player repeats the performance and passes it to the third player. This continues until all the players have skipped the required number of times. The team finishing first wins. Any number of skips may be used, from five to forty.

Pony Relay

The players are arranged in parallel columns of twos, 10 feet apart, abreast of a common starting line. A turning point is established 50 feet in front of each team. At a signal, one of the players making up the first pair, stands behind the other player, puts her head between this player's legs and lifts him so he sits astride the first player's neck. The bottom player is the pony, the top player the jockey. Holding the jockey in position, the pony runs to the turning point where she drops him. The pony stays at the turning point. The jockey runs back to the starting point, where he acts as pony for the third person. This continues until all have been carried forward. Each player serves in turn, first as jockey, and then as pony. The team that first has its last player across the turning point wins.

Potato Relay

The teams are arranged in parallel columns of files, 10 feet apart, and abreast of a common starting line. A circle two feet in diameter is drawn immediately in front of each column. A one foot in diameter circle is drawn 30 feet in front of each column. Three potatoes (or wood blocks or stones) are placed in each circle along the starting line. At a signal, the first runner of each line carries the potatoes one at a time and places them in the farthest circle. Completing the task he returns to the starting line and touches off the second player. The second player, carrying one at a time, carries them back to their original circle. The third player carries them forward again. This continues until all have run. Each potato must be placed in the circle before the next can be taken. The team that first has its last player cross the starting line after finishing the task wins.

Prone Lying Circle Relay

The group is arranged in a large circle, players lying down on their stomachs, facing in and holding hands. Each player has his legs together and projecting straight to the rear. The circle is divided in half. Each half constitutes one team. At a signal, the first player on the left of each team rises and runs to the right about the circle, stepping between the bodies of the lying players as he runs. On being touched, the second player repeats the performance of the first. The third, the fourth, and other players follow, until all have run. The team that finishes and is lying in its original position first wins.

Raised Leg Relay

The teams are arranged in parallel columns of files, 10 feet apart, and abreast of a common line, players standing at normal intervals. A turning point is established 50 feet in front of each column. In this race, the contestants compete in pairs. The first two players of each column stand on one foot and raise the other foot backward. The second player grasps the upraised ankle of the first player. At a signal, these two players, retaining their starting formation, hop to, or around, the turning point and back to the starting line. While they are hopping the third and fourth players get in position at the starting line. At the starting line, the first pair touch off the second pair, who repeat the performance of the first pair. In this manner, the race continues until all have run. The team finishing first wins.

Rescue Relay

The teams are divided in half, and one half of each team stands in parallel columns, abreast of a common line. The other half of each team lies on their backs in line 20 yards in front. The teams should be 20 feet apart. At a signal, the first player of each team at the starting line runs to the first player of his group lying down, picks him up, places him over his shoulders and carries him to the starting line. The player lying on his back must not assist the carrier in any way; he must be dead weight. The second carrier starts forward as the first crosses the starting line, runs to the group in front, and carries the second player back. In this manner, the race continues until all have run. The team returning its last player across the starting line first wins.

Rise and Run Relay

The teams are arranged in parallel columns of files, 10 feet apart, abreast of a common line. A turning point is established 40 feet in front of each column. One player starts on the turning point in front of each column. This player lies on his back, head toward the column. At a signal, the first player in the column runs forward and tags the player lying in front. Upon being tagged, this player rises to his feet and runs to the starting point, where he tags the next player in the column. In the meantime, the player who tagged him lies down in the same place. As soon as the second player is tagged, he runs forward to the prone player in front. This continues until all have run forward. The team finishing in its original position first wins.

Roll Over Man Relay

The teams are arranged in parallel columns, 10 feet apart, abreast of a common line. One player is 10 feet in front of each column, resting on his hands and knees, side toward the column. This player lowers his hips and bends his arms slightly so he rests close to the ground. At a signal, the entire column moves forward in file formation. Each player in turn places his hands on the ground just at the side of the kneeling player and executes a forward roll over his body. As soon as the roll is completed, the player turns to the right and runs around to the rear of the column, and then moves forward to his original position. The team returning and squatting in its original position first wins.

Rope Climb Relay

One climbing rope is required for each team in this game. Each rope is marked 12 feet from the floor either by a ribbon or chalk and a mat is placed under the rope. The teams are arranged in columns, each team directly behind a rope. At a signal, the first player of each team steps forward and climbs the rope, touches the mark, and drops to the floor. As soon as he hits the floor, the second player, who has previously taken position close to the rope, repeats this performance. Each player in turn follows, starting as soon as his predecessor has hit the floor. Players may start climbing with a jump. The team that has its last player hit the floor first wins.

Rope Skip Relay

The teams are arranged in parallel columns of files, 10 feet apart, abreast of a common line. A turning point is established 60 feet in front of each column. The first player of each column starts with a piece of rope eight-feet long. At a signal, the player with the rope moves forward to, or around, the turning point and returns to the starting line, skipping the rope all the way. At the starting line, he passes the rope to the second player who repeats the performance. Any player who stops skipping must halt and start again before advancing. Each player skips in his turn until all have skipped. The team having its last player cross the starting line first wins.

Run, Toss, and Catch Relay

The teams are arranged in parallel columns of files, 10 feet apart, abreast of a common line. A turning point is established 40 feet in front of each column. The first player of each team starts with four beanbags. At a signal, the player with the beanbags runs forward to the turning point and tosses the bags, one at a time, back to the second player, who has in the meantime stepped up to the line. On catching the fourth bag, the second player runs to the turning point where he tosses the beanbags to the third player. This continues until all have carried them forward. The team having its last player cross the starting line first wins.

Sack Relay

The teams are divided in half. One half of each team stands in a column of files, abreast of a common line, 60 feet to the front facing the first half. The teams should be 10 feet apart. A sack is placed on the ground before the first player of half A of each team. At a signal, this player picks up the sack, steps into it, pulls it up and around his waist and hops forward to half B of his team. Reaching this point, he drops the sack and steps out of it. The first player here steps into the sack, adjusts it, and hops back to the starting line. The second player of half A returns with it. This shuttle continues until all have run. The team that has its last player cross the opposite line first wins.

Sultan Relay

The teams are arranged in parallel columns of twos, 10 feet apart, abreast of a common line. A turning point is established 30 feet in front of each column. Each pair of players joins inside hands. An extra player, preferably a light, fast player (the sultan) stands in front of each column. At a signal, the sultan sits on the folded hands of the first pair in the column, placing his arms about their shoulders. These players carry him forward to the turning point and drop him to the ground. He returns immediately to the starting line where he mounts the joined hands of the second pair in his column. These players carry him forward as the first pair did. This continues—the sultan returning to be carried forward by each pair in the column, until all have run. The team finishing first wins.

Single File Relay

The teams are arranged in columns 10 feet apart, abreast of a common starting line. A turning point is established 100 feet in front of each team. At a signal, each team, maintaining its original formation, runs forward around the turning point and back to the starting line. The players are required to stay in their positions in the line; they are not permitted to pass players in front. The team having its last player across the starting line first wins.

Sitting Circle Relay

The group is arranged in a large circle, players sitting down facing out with legs projecting straight to the front and holding hands. The circle is divided in half, each half forming one team. At a signal, the first player on the left of each team rises and runs around the outside of the circle, running to the right, stepping, as he runs, between the legs of the players sitting. On arriving at the starting point, the runner steps forward, touches the second player, and then sits down in his original position. On being touched the second player repeats the performance of the first. The third, fourth, and others follow in turn until all have run. The team that finishes and is sitting in its original position first wins.

Skipping Relay

The teams are arranged in parallel columns of files, 10 feet apart, abreast of a common line. A turning point is established 60 feet in front of each team. At a signal, the first player of each team skips to, or around, the turning point and back to the starting line. At this point, he touches off the second player, who repeats. The third, fourth, fifth, and other players follow until all have run. The team finishing first wins.

Stake Bowl Relay

The teams are arranged in parallel columns of files, 10 feet apart, abreast of a common line. An Indian club or stake standing on end is placed 40 feet in front of each column. If a wall is available, the columns are arranged so these clubs may be placed abreast of it, five feet from the same. If no wall is available, an extra player from each team stands just beyond each club. A line is drawn half way between the club and the column. This is the throwing line. The first player of each column starts with a ball. At a signal, the first player runs forward to the throwing line. From this point, he attempts to bowl over the club. If he is not successful, he recovers the ball and tries again from the same throwing line. The thrower has three trials. Upon making a successful throw, or completing his third attempt, he sets up the club if it is down, recovers the ball, and passes it to the second player in his column. This player must receive the ball behind the starting line. After receiving it, he runs forward and attempts to bowl over the club, as did the first player. The player beyond the club, if there is one, does nothing more than recover the ball and return it to the thrower. This continues until all have competed. The team having its last player cross the starting line with the ball first wins.

Stepping Stones Relay

The teams are arranged in closed columns of files, 10 feet apart, abreast of a common line. A turning point is established 50 feet in front of each team. Bricks, flat stones, or blocks of wood are placed at varying distances apart, at no point farther than eight feet nor less than two, in a direct line between the starting point and turning point of each team. This should give stepping stones anywhere from two feet to seven feet apart. The stepping stones of each team should occupy the same relative positions. At a signal, the first player of each team runs forward, stepping on the stones to, or around, the turning point and returns to the starting point. The runner must step on each stone on each trip. At the starting point, he touches the second player, who repeats the performance. The third player, the fourth, and the other players, each run in turn until all have run. Any player stepping off, or falling off, a stone must return to the last stone he was on and start again. The team that has its last player cross the starting line first wins.

Stick and Ball Relay

The teams are arranged in parallel columns of files, 10 feet apart, abreast of a common line. A turning point is established 50 feet in front of each team. The first player of each team starts with a ball and a stick about three-feet long. Each places the ball on the starting line. At a signal, each player pushing the ball before him, runs to the turning point and back to the starting line. At this point, each passes the stick to the second member of his team, who repeats. The players are not allowed to hit the ball, but must push it by sliding the stick on the floor and scooping it along. This continues until all have run. The team finishing first wins.

Stiff Knee Jumping Relay

The teams are arranged in parallel columns of files, 10 feet apart, abreast of a common line. A turning point is established 30 feet in front of each team. At a signal, the first player on each team, with his arms folded on his chest, knees rigid, and feet close together jumps forward with short rapid toe springs to, or around, the turning point and back to the starting line. Here he touches off the second player, who repeats. This continues until all have run. The team finishing first wins.

Straddle Ball Relay

The teams are arranged in parallel columns of files, 10 feet apart, abreast of a common line, the players in each column three feet apart. All of the players spread their legs. The first player in each team starts with a ball. At a signal, the player with the ball rolls it back between the legs of his teammates. If necessary, other players in the column may help roll it along. The last player receives it, carries it to the head of the column, and sends it through again. After rolling the ball, the player takes a position with feet spread in front of the column. Each player in turn carries the ball forward until all have carried it. The team arriving at its original formation first wins.

Take and Put Relay

The teams are arranged in parallel lines, 10 feet apart, players standing five feet apart, with feet spread. Ten objects (e.g., dumbbells, beanbags, or stones) are placed to the left of the left end player of each team. At a signal, the first player of each group picks up the objects, one at a time, with his left hand, transfers them to the right hand, and places them on the floor to his right. As soon as the first object is placed, the second player picks it up and places it to his right. This continues until all have been transferred to the right end of the line. The team placing its last object on the floor to the right first wins.

Variations:
The players stand 10 feet apart and each player marks his position, using a large stone or a piece of chalk. At a signal, the first player of each team picks up one object and runs and hands it to the second player, who runs and hands it to the third, and so on until it is passed down the line to the last player, who places it at his feet. As soon as the first player has handed his object to the second, he runs back to his position and picks up another. No player is allowed to step to the left of his own mark, or to the right of the mark of the player on his right. Also, each object must be passed from hand to hand and not thrown.

Any player dropping an object must pick it up and pass it before he can accept another object. In this manner the running and passing continues until all the objects have been placed at the last player's feet.

Tandem Relay

The teams are arranged in parallel columns of files, 10 feet apart, abreast of a common line. A turning point is established 40 feet in front of each column. The players of each column are assembled in pairs. The rear player of each pair circles the front player's waist with his arms and clasps hands. At a signal, the leading pair, maintaining their original position, runs forward to, or around, the turning point and back to the starting line. At this point, the front player tags one of the next pair, who are now ready at the starting line. The second pair repeats the performance of the first. This continues until all have run. The team finishing first wins.

Additional Comments:
- The leader should teach the players to circle the front players' waists with both arms and clasp hands without putting undue pressure on the soft tissue of the abdomen *or* have players hold the player in front of them with their hands on the bony structure of the sides of the hips.

Tap Top Relay

The teams are arranged in parallel column of files, 10 feet apart, abreast of a common line. Two Indian clubs are placed in front of each team, one 20 feet in front, and one 40 feet in front. At a signal, the first player of each team runs forward to the second club (40 feet), picks it up, turns it over, touches its top to the floor, sets it up, runs back to the first club (20 feet), repeats this again, and then runs to the starting line. At the starting line, he touches off the second player, who repeats this performance. The others follow in turn until all have competed. The team finishing first wins.

Target Relay

The teams are arranged in closed columns, 10 feet apart, abreast of a common line. A one-foot-square base is established 50 feet in front of each column. If a wall is available, the columns are arranged so these bases are abreast of it, five feet distant from the same. If no wall is available, a player from each team stands beyond each of the bases. One player stands on each base. The throwing line is a line 10 feet in front of the columns. The first player of each column starts with a ball.

At a signal, the first player runs forward to the throwing line. From this point, he attempts to hit the player standing on the base. If he is not successful, he recovers the ball and tries again from the same throwing line. The thrower has three trials. Upon making a successful throw, or completing his third attempt, he recovers the ball and passes it to the second player in the column. This player must receive it in back of the starting line. After receiving the ball, he runs forward and repeats the efforts of the first player. The player on the base is an independent figure. He must keep one foot on the base, otherwise he may do anything he can to prevent being hit. Failure to keep one foot on the base scores the same as a hit for the thrower. The player beyond the base, if there is one, does nothing more than recover the ball and return it to the thrower. The game continues until all have thrown. The team that has its last player finish and hold the ball in back of the starting line first wins.

Three-Legged Relay

The teams are arranged in parallel columns of twos, 10 feet apart, abreast of a common line. A turning point is established 60 feet in front of each column. The first pair of players on each team places a belt about the inside legs, just below the knees (a rope may be used), binding the two legs together very tightly. At a signal, the bound pair runs forward to, or around, the turning point and returns. On reaching the starting line, they halt, remove the belt, and pass it on to the second pair. The second pair, upon receiving the belt fasten it about their inside legs, and repeat the performance of the first pair. This continues until each pair has run. The team having its last pair cross the starting line first wins.

Undress and Dress Relay

The teams are arranged in parallel columns of files, 10 feet apart, abreast of a common line. A turning point is established 80 feet in front of each column. At a signal, the first player in each column runs forward five paces, halts, removes and deposits his shoes, runs forward five more paces, halts and deposits his hat, runs forward five more paces, halts and deposits his coat, runs forward five more paces and deposits his necktie, and then runs forward to, or around, the turning point and returns by the same route, picking up each article of clothing and putting it on as he comes to it. Players are not allowed to remove or put on clothing while running. Each piece must be completely adjusted before reaching the starting line. At the starting line, he touches off the next player who repeats. This continues until all have run. The team that has its last player return across the starting line first wins.

Variety Pass Relay

The teams are arranged in parallel lines 10 feet apart, players standing 10 feet apart. A basketball, a stone, a dumbbell, and a playground ball are placed at the feet of the player to the left of each team. At a signal, the first player picks up the dumbbell and tosses it to the second player, and then picks up the basketball and bounces it to him, picks up the playground ball and rolls it to him, and picks up the stone and runs and hands it to him. The second player, upon receiving each object, places it at his feet. Upon receiving the stone, he places it at his feet, and then proceeding in the same manner as did the first, transfers them to the third who, in a similar manner, passes them on to the fourth, and so on to the end of the line. The last player, upon receiving them places them at his feet. The team that puts its last article on the floor in front of its last player first wins.

Waist Carry Relay

The teams are arranged in parallel columns of files, 10 feet apart, abreast of a common line. A turning point is established 40 feet in front of each team. The first player in each team leans slightly forward and the second player lies across the small of his back. Then the first player puts one arm around the second player's legs and one arm about his back, and thus lifts the second player from the floor. At a signal, the first player in each team, carrying the second player in this manner, runs forward to the turning point. There the carrier drops the rider to the floor. The first player remains there. The second player runs back to the starting line, picks up the third player, as previously outlined, and carries him to the turning point. This continues until all have been carried forward. The player who rides down runs back and carries the next player down. The team finishing first wins.

Walking Relay

The teams are arranged in parallel columns of files, 10 feet apart, abreast of a common line. A turning point is established 60 feet in front of each column. At a signal, the first player of each team walks forward to, or around, the turning point and back to the starting line. In walking, a player must place the heel of the advancing foot on the floor before the toe of the trailing foot is lifted. At the starting line, the walker touches off the second player who repeats. This continues until all have walked. The team finishing first wins.

Zigzag Hopping Relay

The teams are arranged in parallel columns of files, 10 feet apart, abreast of a common line. A turning point is established 40 feet in front of each column. Seven Indian clubs are placed at intervals of five feet in a direct line between the starting line and the last five feet from the turning point. One player from each team stands at the turning point. At a signal, the first player from each team hops forward to the turning point, traveling alternately to the left and the right of the clubs. At the turning point the runner and player stationed there, link elbows and run around each other twice and release. The player who had just hopped out from the column remains at the turning point. The player who had been stationed there hops back to the starting line, zigzagging to alternate sides of the clubs. At the starting line, he touches off the second player, who zigzagging to the left and right, hops to the turning point. Any player knocking down a club must set it in place before proceeding. He must do this while standing on one foot. This continues until all have hopped forward. The player who was stationed in front at the beginning, hops out and relieves the last player. The team having its last player cross the starting line first wins.

Zigzag Running Relay

The teams are arranged in parallel columns of files, 10 feet apart, abreast of a common line. Eight Indian clubs are placed in a column directly in front of each team, clubs standing one foot apart, the first club 10 feet from the line. At a signal, the first player of each team runs forward to the clubs, and, traveling alternately to the left and right of the clubs, runs to the farthest club, circles it, and traveling alternately to the left and right again, returns to the starting line. Here he touches off the second player, who repeats this performance. This continues until all have competed. The team finishing first wins.

Gym-Scooter Snake Relay

The teams are arranged in file formation. The first player of each team lays on his belly on the scooter. The relay is started behind a line and the players must go to a second line 50 feet away. They use their hands and arms for propulsion by pulling themselves. When they reach the second line, they must turn around and come back and the second player in line goes. The teams should be limited to five or six players.

Gym-Scooter Wheelbarrow Relay

The teams are arranged in file formation. The first player on each team lays on the scooter with it under the lower part of his chest. The next player in line grasps the first player's feet and pushes him down and back. The player that did the pushing then gets on the scooter and the next player in line does the pushing. The teams should be limited to five to eight players.

Two-Legged Gym-Scooter Relay

The teams are arranged in file formation. Each team has one scooter. Players sit on the scooter and push with both legs. Each player must go down and back. The distance for the relay shouldn't be less than 30 feet in length.

Gym-Scooter Train Relay

The teams are arranged in file formation. This game requires two or more scooters per team. Players sit on scooters and put their legs around the persons in front of them, thus forming a train. They propel themselves with their hands. There are many different ways to play this game, so the leader may use the one that best fits his situation. If the group is small and enough scooters are available, everyone can be on a scooter. Different players can go each time or the players may continue to move up one scooter at a time until everyone has gone from the back to the front.

Games for the Beach

Ostrich Tag

This can be played with any number of people, and the rules can be changed at the whim of whoever is IT. In this instance, anyone may be tagged unless he stands on his left leg, his right leg in the air, his right arm underneath the right leg and his left hand holding his nose. Ostrich tag can be played either on the shore or in the water.

Poison

A balloon is anchored with a rock and string in waist-high water, and the players form a ring around it. The object is to make a member of the circle touch the balloon. When he comes in contact with it, he is poisoned and he must drop out. The last one untouched is the winner.

Chinese Chickens

Equipment for this game calls for 12 (or 18) beach objects, such as sandals, suntan oil, and shells. These "chickens" are laid out six to a row, in two or three rows (depending on the number of teams competing). They should be placed a foot and a half apart, between parallel lines. Each player in turn hops on one foot, picks up the object farthest away, and then hops back to the starting point. He puts the chicken down, and then hops after the next one. If he steps on the lines, uses two hands, drops the chicken, or hops more than once between two of them, the next player in line takes over. The team that picks up all the chickens first is the winner.

Balloon Inflating

Contestants are given balloons. Each in turn takes a deep breath, ducks underwater, tries to inflate the balloon underwater, and sees how high it will expand above the surface.

Shoreside Leapfrog

This game is one way to get teenagers or adults into the water. It is played partly on land and partly in waist-deep water. The players leap toward the water, getting in deeper and deeper. Anyone who does not clear the hurdle is eliminated.

Bronco

This game is also known as Chicken Fight. Two players form a horse and rider by one player sitting on the other player's shoulders. Then two riders try to unhorse each other by pushing or pulling until one rider loses his balance. If this is played in teams, the side with a rider still on his horse is the winner. Since this game can be very rough, it should be played in waist-deep water with close supervision.

Variations:
- As soon as the top player is in place, the bronco tries to throw him. The rider who sticks longest wins.

Splash Ball

For this game a large rubber ball that will float is the only equipment needed. The players kneel or sit in a circle in shallow water, with only the ball in the center. By splashing with their hands, they try to push the ball to the others in the circle. Players are eliminated if they touch the ball.

Water Pullaway

The player who is IT is stationed at a designated spot in the shallow water, 10 feet from the rest of the players, who are standing in a line. The player at the head of the line tries to run around IT and return to home base. If caught, he is IT.

Stunt Tag

One player is IT and the others scatter through waist-deep water. IT calls out a part of the body which must be out of the water to secure immunity from being tagged. For example: "One foot out," "Knee out," or "Big toe out."

Suggestions for a Successful Party

A few games hurriedly selected and executed may suffice occasionally for a party, but such a procedure cannot long endure. Group fun should be well-planned and well-directed. There is no other way for a successful party. The following suggestions will help a leader or host in conducting a successful event:

1. Decide upon the kind of party you are going to have. If it is to be a seasonal theme, patriotic, prenuptial, or any kind of special party, build the entire program around that central theme. Obtain ideas from games and party books for these special occasions.

2. Detailed planning and preparation should be made in advance of the party. Select games to be played according to the age group and kind of party. Strike a medium between the very strenuous and less active games. Even young people have the capacity for becoming tired and losing interest if the games tend to lean in one direction, either too active or too quiet. Equalize the running and sitting games. Where the group is mixed, even with very little tots, have some games in which all can play. Neglect no one.

3. Know what you are going to do. Unless you have a definite program and a clear conception of every activity from the beginning to the end of the program, be prepared to witness severe criticism beyond your hearing. To have a list of games on a sheet of paper is not sufficient. *Know those games.* Have each in mind and so thoroughly learned that you will know every detail, and you will be able to interpret each game so concisely, clearly, and consistently that the players will definitely understand what to do.

4. Avoid ambiguous speech. While you may have a very clear conception of your vocabulary, there are those in the average party who can understand only simple words. Use simple language and explain each game.

5. Ignore no one. The hesitant, the latecomers, old people, and children—indeed, everyone, regardless of age—like to play. Endeavor to make each person feel important to the success of the party. The aged and the young are sensitive to neglect. Permit no one to go home with injured feelings.

6. Avoid monotony. Stop the game and begin another when the players are enjoying it the most.

7. When necessary, provide prizes. But do not practice giving rewards. Play should be enjoyed for the fun of it, and not for the pay of it. Cooperative endeavor without continuous material reward makes for greater satisfaction.

8. Leave nothing to chance. Have all material for the party and each game arranged in advance.

Games for Special Occasions

President's Day

Pictures of Presidents are hung about the room with their names covered or omitted. Each player writes down the name of each President. Highest score wins.

Presidential Quotations

The leader should select famous quotations from Washington and Lincoln (or any President) in advance. Each player writes down the author in numerical order as the leader reads each quotation.

Presidential Birthplaces

The leader selects birthplaces of the Presidents and conducts the game as Presidential Quotations.

Valentine's Day Post Office

The leader will cut out paper hearts in various colors, one for each person present, and pass them out to the players. Each person writes some valentine greeting on a heart and his name at the bottom. Each person deposits the heart in the "post office" box in the center of the room. One player is blindfolded and this player draws hearts out of the box one at a time, while another player reads each, including the author's name.

Additional Comments:
This may be adapted to birthday, Christmas, New Year's, and other parties.

Valentine Party Getting Acquainted

The leader should acquire an equal number of inscribed candy hearts for each player. *Yes* and *no* are two forbidden words, neither of which can be used without a penalty. At a signal, the players move about conversing with others hoping to cause each person contacted to say *yes* or *no*. Every time a forbidden word is used, the player who said the word must forfeit a heart to the person with whom he was talking. At the conclusion of the game, the player with the most hearts wins.

Irish Sayings Getting Acquainted

The leader should prepare slips of paper with Irish sayings, but leave enough space for a person's name after the paper has been cut diagonally. The leader passes out sections to players. Each player writes her name on her section, then finds the player who possesses the section with the rest of the saying.

Humorous Band

In advance of the party, the leader may select people to form a band using an ensemble of kitchenware or other items which will cause a laughable situation:

- bass drum—dish pan or basin,
- cymbals—two kettle lids,
- conductor's baton—wooden rolling pin or meat cleaver,
- accordion—toy reproduction or collapsible hat rack,
- fife—long knife sharpener,
- snare drum—frying pan, and
- trombone—sliding curtain rod.

Vanishing Egg

The leader or magician will prepare four eggs on a tray—two good raw eggs (marked) and two eggs carefully pierced, with the contents blown out. The magician announces that she is going to make raw eggs disappear within somebody's hat. She picks up a good egg, drops it by mistake so that it spills, and apologizes. Then, with many flourishes, she picks up a blown egg, holds it inside the hat, and breaks it. The magician goes through the motions of emptying the egg into the hat, and then places the broken shell on the table. This process is repeated with the other blown egg. Finally she says, "I will make the eggs disappear," and returns the hat in perfect condition.

Tin Can Alley

Two contestants each stand on two tin cans at a starting point. They race to the other side of room, standing on one can while the other is moved ahead (see Crossing the River).

Musical Chairs

This starts with one less chair than there are players. When the music stops, all rush to the chairs. Any player not finding a chair is eliminated. Another chair is removed and this repeats until a winner has occurred.

Egg Cracker

A few eggs are placed a foot apart in a line on the floor. One player removes her shoes and socks and rehearses the technique of stepping over each egg. The player is blindfolded and the eggs are replaced by oyster crackers. With proper "guidance" by either the leader or another group member, she is eventually made to step on a pile of four oyster crackers.

Backward Spelling Bee

The leader will prepare a list of words that the players will spell backwards.

Thanksgiving Party Getting Acquainted

This is an icebreaker for a large gathering. Each player tries to find a person at the party whose name (first or last) begins with one of the letters from the word *Thanksgiving* (or whichever theme or occasion is being celebrated). For example:

> T—Theresa
> H—Hillary
> A—Ann
> N—Nancy
> K—Ken
> S—Smith
> G—George
> I—Irving
> V—Victoria
> I—Irene
> N—Nathan
> G—Gloria

The first player completing the word wins.

Thanksgiving Menu

This is a paper-and-pencil game made by placing well-known food advertisements about the room. The trademarks or names on the advertisements are removed or covered. The players are supposed to make a menu mentioning the brand, such as Del Monte peaches and Campbell's soup, according to the numbers appearing in the advertisements. The advertisements may be cut from magazines or newspapers.

Christmas Cut-up Puzzle

The leader will have several well-known pictures relative to the season cut in pieces and deposited in boxes. He will pass out the boxes to groups, supplying glue or tape and a cardboard or paper upon which to glue or tape the pictures. The group assembling its picture correctly in the shortest time wins the game.

Spider Web

Instead of the traditional grab bag, the leader stretches and intertwines cord strings from one room to another with a gift at the end of each string. The guests trace out a string apiece. Cords may be suspended from the ceiling.

Animal Twists

Untwist the words. This can be played individually or in pairs. The participant who untwists each word correctly first wins. The list may be expanded to include more animals or it may be done using categories other than animals, e.g., holidays, states, cereal, cities, or football team names.

Twisted Word	Answer
1. Shore	horse
2. Tassy cup	pussy cat
3. Areb	bear
4. Kendoy	donkey
5. Sinob	bison
6. Kastrum	muskrat
7. Chowdouck	woodchuck
8. Allam	llama
9. Present	serpent
10. Talligora	alligator
11. Hungrydeo	greyhound
12. Kacopec	peacock
13. Gip	pig
14. Somsoup	opossum

Famous People

Individually, in pairs, or in groups, the participants will identify the famous person by his or her famous prop. This list can easily be expanded using sports figures, movie stars, and cartoon characters.

Prop	Answer
1. Foot print	Robinson Crusoe
2. Silver lamp	Aladdin
3. Kite	Ben Franklin
4. Apple	William Tell
5. Muddy cloak	Sir Walter Raleigh
6. Wolf	Little Red Riding Hood
7. Spider web	Robert Bruce
8. Hatchet	George Washington
9. Glass slipper	Cinderella
10. Slingshot	David
11. Looking glass	Alice in Wonderland
12. Steamboat	Fulton

Name Me

The name of an animal, tree, or flower is pinned on the back of each guest. Each person tries to learn from other players what he is. As he asks various questions, they make ambiguous replies. Each question should be answered relative to the description of the animal, tree, or flower, but not so as to make identification easy. Three questions may be asked of each person. If unsuccessful, they must part and endeavor to learn their identities from other players.

Observations

The host should prepare a tray with various objects in advance of the party. The arrangement is uncovered, permitting the players to observe the articles for a brief period, and then covered again. Then the host passes out paper and pencils, and has each player note the articles. The player with the highest score wins.

Penny Contest

Each player or team has a Lincoln "wheat" penny, paper, and pencil. Each player writes the answers to the following based upon what is on the penny:

1. Find a fruit	date
2. Find flowers	tulips (two lips)

3. Find a bridge	bridge of nose
4. Find the common word of an egotist	I (eye)
5. Find a weapon of punishment	lash
6. Find an animal	hare (hair)
7. Find part of a hill	brow
8. Find part of a corn stalk	ear
9. Find part of a railroad track	tie
10. Find a messenger	one cent (one sent)
11. Find a country	United States of America
12. Find a motto	In God We Trust
13. Find what all people love	Liberty
14. Find part of an automobile tire	the rim
15. Find something belonging to every animal	coat
16. Find a part of a man's pipe	stem
17. Find part of a tree	leaves
18. Find something peculiar to a goat	beard
19. Find something all dogs should have	collar
20. What is possessed by meddlesome people?	cheek

Famous American Shrines

The leader will prepare questions on slips of paper for the guests to answer. A definite time should be set for this game, such as five to ten minutes.

1. Where is the cradle of liberty?	Boston, MA
2. Where is Ben Franklin's home?	Philadelphia, PA
3. Where is Concord Bridge?	Concord, MA
4. Where is Plymouth Rock?	Plymouth, MA
5. Where is George Washington's Tomb?	Mt. Vernon, VA
6. Where is Betsy Ross's house?	Philadelphia, PA
7. Where is George Washington's birthplace?	Williamsburg, VA
8. Where is the Gettysburg Battlefield?	Gettysburg, PA
9. Where is the Lincoln Memorial?	Washington, DC
10. Where is Independence Hall?	Philadelphia, PA
11. Where is Valley Forge?	Valley Forge, PA
12. Where is the Statue of Liberty?	New York Bay
13. Where is the Smithsonian Institute?	Washington, DC
14. Where is the Football Hall of Fame?	Canton, OH
15. Where is the Washington Monument?	Washington, DC
16. Where is Grant's Tomb?	New York City
17. Where is Lincoln's birthplace?	New Hodgensville, KY
18. Where is the Lincoln home?	Springfield, IL

19. Where is McKinley's Tomb?   Canton, OH
20. Where is Old South Church?   Boston, MA

Pass the Hatchet

The leader will make a cardboard hatchet. The players are in a circle. At the beginning of the piano music, the hatchet is passed from player to player. The player having the hatchet when the music stops must drop from the game. The same applies to any player dropping the hatchet.

Getting Acquainted

The leader should cut out either small hatchets or colonial hats or large cherries from red construction paper. The items are then cut into two sections. One section is placed in a box for boys, and one for girls. The boys sit in one row while the girls sit in another row, the two rows facing each other. Each contestant is given a part. At a signal, the players find partners by matching the part of the object in his or her hand. When a partner is found, the players must exchange names and two interests or hobbies.

Treasure Hunt

The host hides small objects about the room for the players to find.

Another Ice Breaker

The hostess asks each guest to bring a childhood snapshot of himself. She mixes them up and redistributes them. When a player finds the person who belongs to the snapshot, he has found his dinner partner (or partner in a game or sport).

Balloon Dance

Each dancer has a balloon securely tied to an ankle with six or eight inches of play in the string. When the music begins, all dancers are paired up, grab hands, and attempt to burst each other's balloon. Any player with a burst balloon sits down, and the dance continues.

Football With an Egg

Place an egg (either a plastic one or one that has had its contents blown out) on a table and let the crowd go to it. The players try to blow the egg off the table anywhere on the opponent's half.

Mirror Writing

This requires two pieces of paper with four dots to form corners of a square, pencil, and mirror. At a signal, each of the two contestants tries to draw the side and diagonals of his square by looking in the mirror which is held or set to reflect the paper. A folded newspaper may be held over the contestants' hands to relieve any temptations to look. Each contestant attempts to complete the design looking only at the reflection in the mirror.

Favorites

Each player makes a list of 10 selected favorites such as favorite boy or girl, food, TV shows, games, and sport teams. The leader collects the lists. Then the lists are read aloud, without mentioning names. If the name of the writer is guessed, he must own up.

Personality Ratings

The group selects five or six categories such as sense of humor, brains, disposition, good looks, sex appeal, and sports skills. Each player takes a sheet of paper and rates himself (on a scale from 1 to 10) based on what he thinks he honestly deserves. Then the papers are turned over and passed around. Each player puts down what he thinks the others should rate. The host reads aloud first the player's personal rating and then the group's average of the player.

New Year Reverie

The leader will make a scrapbook for each guest, or one book for a definite number of players, from wrapping paper with the pages tied together with cord string. Each book is divided into chapters which deal with either community or national events. Each individual or group makes a pictorial history from magazine clippings. (The leader will provide old magazines, scissors, and other items.) Examples of chapter headings on national events include political events, happenings in sports, and important people. The following subjects should be included for individual history: birth; babyhood; childhood; games or interests; and college, school, and/or job. The books may be displayed after completion.

New Year Resolutions

The host will provide guests with pencil and paper and instruct each person to write a name at the top and fold the paper over so as to conceal the writing and to pass the paper to the next person. Each person writes a resolution, folds the paper, and passes it. The next person writes the reason for the resolution. The next person writes the means by which the resolution will be kept. The next person writes the only condition under which the resolution will be broken. After each statement has been written, the paper should be folded and passed. Upon the completion of the condition statement the papers are passed again. Then each is unfolded and read in turn.

Bubble Blowing Contest

Each guest is given a clay pipe or wand tied with a green ribbon. The leader supplies a big bowl of soapy water and has each guest in turn come up and blow as large a bubble as he can, making a careful note of the winner. Then they start over again and each guest blows as small a bubble as he can and the leader notes the winner. The next is the highest bubble, then the most bubbles from one wetting of the pipe or wand. The winners of each of these contests then competes in the finals, and the winner of that is awarded a prize appropriate for the occasion.

Blowing Cherries

This is a good activity to use when things seem to be going slow. A string is stretched lengthwise across the room of the floor, dividing it into two fields. The boys are on one side and the girls on the other. A giant cherry (a big red balloon) is thrown into the air from the center of the line. When it comes down, each side, by blowing only, endeavors to cause it to touch either an opponent or the floor on the opposite side of the line. The side successful in doing so gets a score, and the balloon is again tossed in the air. Nobody may step over the line nor touch the balloon or be touched by it, or it goes to the opposing side. The side which first gets a score of 10 wins. The losers will have so much fun that no consolation prize is necessary.

About the United States

Each of the following questions can be answered by the abbreviation of one of the 50 states:

1.	Which state is the cleanest?	(Wash)ington
2.	Which state is the most religious?	(Mass)achusetts
3.	Which state saved Noah and his family?	(Ark)ansas
4.	Which state is a physician?	Maryland (MD)
5.	Which state is in poor health?	(Ill)inois
6.	Which state is an exclamation?	Ohio (OH)
7.	Which state is a parent?	Pennsylvania (PA)

8. Which state is used to cut long grass?   Missouri (MO)
9. Which state is a number?   (Ten)nessee
10. Which state is a metal in its natural formation?   (Ore)gon

Cap Pass Relay

The teams are arranged in parallel lines 10 feet apart, players standing four feet apart. All of the players of each team are given a stick three-feet long. The players grasp the stick at one end and hold it upright. The first players of each team starts with a cap. At a signal, the player with the cap places it on top of his stick. He then transfers it to the second player's stick. The second player transfers it to the third, and so on, until the cap is passed to the last player in the line. All transfers must be made without the use of the hands. If the cap falls to the floor, it must be picked up with the stick, without the use of the hands. The team placing its cap on the stick of the last player first wins.

Potato Jab

Each contestant has a potato and a fork. Each tosses the potato in the air and attempts to catch it on the prongs of the fork. It will be necessary to throw the potato quite high in order to cause it to stick. Contestants are given three attempts; each successful attempt scores one point.

Annie Oakley

Two tin cans are set about two feet apart on a log. The two teams stand on the throwing line in any convenient location, each trying to throw stones and knock over the opponent's can. When this happens, the successful team gets one point. If a can is knocked over in error by the wrong team, it counts against the thrower.

Holiday Fortune

This is an entertaining game adaptable for any holiday party and the necessary fortunes add to the decorations for the room. A cord is stretched across the room wherever convenient and as many cardboard hearts (or other appropriate holiday item) as there are guests are hung from the cord. Each heart has a fortune written on it. Each fortune may require the guest to do some simple feat. The success of the game depends on the humor and clever feats of the fortunes.

The guests are blindfolded, one at a time, and each selects a fortune. Then each reads aloud the fortune he has chosen. Each guest should remove his fortune from the cord.

Geography

This game is for any number of players. A player starts the game by naming a geographical location. The player next in line must then name a place that begins with the last letter of the previously named word. The places named by different players do not have to be of one type, but may be cities, rivers, lakes, or countries, just as long as they are on the map. For instance, the first player might say, "Europe," the second, "England," and the third, "Danube." A player who is unable to name a place within a specified time is eliminated until a new game begins. The player who stays in longest wins.

Letter Fortune

Each player cuts letters from a newspaper and puts them in water. The ones that float should form a name. This will be the name of the player's future sweetheart.

TKB

This game can be adapted for almost any occasion. For instance, Christmas is printed twice vertically like this:

C	__	__	S
H	__	__	A
R	__	__	M
I	__	__	T
S	__	__	S
T	__	__	I
M	__	__	R
A	__	__	H
S	__	__	C

The players are given 10 or 15 minutes in which to fill in the letters in each line that will spell a bona fide word. Any word will do, just as long as it begins and ends with the designated letters.

Birthplace Bodements

Each player writes down the name of his birthplace on a slip of paper. The slips are then gathered up, shuffled, and redistributed. Now each works out a fortune of as many words as there are letters in the name of the town on the slip he draws. For example, should the town be Peterborough, the fortune teller might advise: "Persistently eat turnips either raw, boiled, or roasted or untold grief happens." The one who finds Detroit on his slip might prophesy: "Date extraordinary truly, really occurs in time." The one who was born in Erie would be delighted to learn there would be: "Enormous riches inherited eventually."

After five or ten minutes have been allowed for writing the fortunes, the slips are exchanged and all in turn, read off the birthplace on the slip he now has. The one whose birthplace it is signifies that fact, and then hears his fortune read (and let us hope the golden fortunes come true and the bad ones are just bunk).

At the end, a vote is taken and the best fortune declared. Then the one who wrote it may claim the prize for making the cleverest of his material.

Rose and Lemons

One girl in the group starts with an artificial rose and one man starts with a lemon. The girl will pass the rose as quickly as possible to another girl, who will hand it on to a third, and so forth. In the same way the men are to keep the lemon moving. At the end of two or three minutes of rapid passing the leader blows his whistle. The girl who holds the rose when the whistle is blown and the man with the lemon are called to the front of the room. The leader hands the man a small box of candy with instructions to present it to the lady. As soon as he has done this, he is given a bill for the candy and told that he is expected to pay for it, since he had the pleasure of presenting the gift. (The leader should secure a bona fide bill when he buys the candy.) Naturally, this trick should not be used more than once with the same crowd.

Identification

The leader will place the objects listed on a table. Each guest is given a sheet of paper with the phrases telling what he must look for. The one with the most correct answers is the winner.

1.	Hidden tears	onion
2.	Bygone days	old calendar
3.	A drive through the woods	nail in wood
4.	We part to meet again	scissors
5.	Flower of the family	flour
6.	Tax on tea	tacks, tea
7.	Home of Burns	iron
8.	The greatest bet ever made	alphabet
9.	Way-worn traveler	shoe
10.	My own native	sand
11.	Ruins of China	dish
12.	Broken heart	paper heart (ripped)
13.	Sweet sixteen	16 candy mints

14. The four seasons	four spices
15. Switch tenders	bobby pins
16. A line from home	clothesline
17. Something to adore	key
18. A perfect foot	ruler
19. Going to be licked	envelope
20. A study of the head	cabbage
21. Book that was never read	book of matches

Independence Day

Each player gets a paper with the following printed on it:

1. Henceforth, I declare my freedom of _____.
2. Because _____.
3. And I resolve to _____.
4. As _____.
5. On _____.

Each person writes in what he frees himself of, and folds the paper over. He passes the paper to the right and that player fills in number 2, stating the reason, without knowing, of course, what the player to his left has declared. The papers are folded each time, number 3 being a new resolution, number 4 the place, and number 5 the time. After all the spaces are filled, the papers are unfolded and read. There will be some sidesplitting combinations.

Abbreviation Letter

The leader says, "Name an insect, a tree, an animal," and so on as word clues. The players answer by using letters of the alphabet that make the word. For example:

Clue	Answer
An insect	B
Not difficult	EZ
A creeping vine	IV
A foe	NME
A number	AT
An Indian's home	TP
A girl's name	KT
All right	OK
To behold	C

Mystery Games

In these games the leader needs a confederate who knows the trick or system used in each one. The confederate leaves the room and while he is out the group decides upon some magic objects. When he returns, he tells which object was selected without any apparent signal from the leader or others. The other players try to guess how the confederate learns which object to pick. When a person thinks that he has discovered the trick, he takes the confederate's place. Frequently it develops that the person's idea is all wrong. The confederate then goes out again. If the person is right, however, he may take the confederate's place until someone else guesses the trick.

Telepathy

Four objects are placed on the floor or four rectangles are marked on the blackboard. When the confederate is out of the room the group selects one of the four objects. The leader then calls the confederate in and asks him which object was chosen. He may pretend to take great care, studying each object in detail first. Later he may give the correct one from some distance, even from outside the room, or blindfolded. The signal is given by the leader in recalling the confederate. Both players have memorized a word or phrase in connection with each article as follows:

OK	All Ready
All Right	Come in

Therefore, if the group selects the upper right object, the leader would call, "All ready," and then the confederate upon returning would point or name the upper right-hand object.

This and That

A player and his partner select four objects, two situated above the others, or they place four objects on the corners of a square. Secretly they agree to name each object as follows:

This	This One
That	That One

The player then leaves the room or covers his eyes, stating that he will guess which one his partner and the group have chosen. When the choice has been made the partner begins to ask questions. He indicates the right object by using its right name when pointing to it. For example, he may ask when he points to the upper left object, "Is it that?" The player answers, "No," because the right name is *this*. His partner then asks "Is it this one?" The player replies, "Yes," because his partner named it by its right name when he pointed to it.

The game may be more baffling if the player and his partner agree that after a certain number of questions or repetitions of the game the names of the objects may be reversed. Still later, the chosen objects can be indicated by wrong names instead of right ones.

Red, White, and Blue

While the confederate is out of the room the group selects some object in the room, possibly something worn by one of the players. On the confederate's return, the leader points to any object and the confederate says, "No," until the right object is pointed out. The signal is given when the leader points to something red. The confederate knows that the next object pointed to will be the one selected by the group. The next time the confederate returns, the signal is something white; the third time it is something blue. That is why the game is known to the leader and confederate, but not to the group, as Red, White and Blue. It is similar to, but more complicated than, Black Magic in which the signal is to mention something black, just before the correct article.

Jamboree

As the confederate leaves the room he places four fingers on the door jamb, to signal the leader that he, the confederate, will say yes when the leader points to the fourth article. The group then picks any article and the confederate answers no to each. The fourth article pointed to must be the one the group decided on, and when the leader points to it the confederate says, "Yes." The signaling should be varied from one to five fingers and be done very unobtrusively.

Tom Thumb

Three objects are placed in front of the leader, one of which is selected by the group while the confederate is out of the room. Upon returning, the confederate pretends to make a difficult decision, and then names the correct article. The leader has signaled him with his thumbs. His hands are folded in his lap and very quietly he crosses his right thumb over his left thumb to indicate the article on the right, his left thumb over the right to indicate the article on the left, and his thumbs parallel to indicate the center article.

Mind Your Questions

The leader chooses four objects. Before the game starts, the leader and his confederate number the articles mentally from one to four. As the game begins, the confederate leaves the room as in previous games. When the group has selected one of the objects, and the confederate returns, the leader gives him the signal by asking any question, starting with a one-letter word if the first article is selected, a two-letter word for the second, three-letter word for the third, and four-letter word for the fourth.

Mental Magic

The group selects a number. When the confederate returns, with or without a blindfold, he stands behind the leader, places his hands lightly on the leader's temple or jaws and gets, by "mental telepathy," the number chosen. The leader makes the mysterious thought waves by clenching his teeth slightly. If the number is 621, the leader clenches his jaws six times, pauses, clenches them twice, pauses, and then clenches them once. Zero is indicated by 10 presses.

No Legs to Stand on

The signal is given by the leader in his first question by indicating whether the object has legs or not. If it has, he mentions then only objects which have no legs, until the correct one which has legs. If the article does not have legs, only articles with legs are mentioned after the first one until the article chosen is pointed to.

Hypnotizing

The leader tells the rest of the players that he can hypnotize his partner and he will do anything the players want him to do. Then the partner leaves the room. The leader tells the other players that they may suggest anything for his partner to do, but it must be expressed in one word, like walk, run, laugh, cry, or read. The leader calls his partner back into the room and has him sit in a chair.

The leader tells his partner to close his eyes and then he massages his forehead with the thumbs stroking in rhythm. If this game is done right the partner will respond to what the other players suggested. The leader spells out the work on his partner's forehead. *A* is one stroke, *B* is two strokes, and so on. To divide up the words the leader should pause before he goes on to the next letter of the alphabet.

The Seer Tells All

A slip of paper is given to each player. Each player writes a question on her slip of paper. The slips are collected by the seer's helper and placed in a hat. The seer sits several feet in front of the players and "tells all."

Solution:
The helper takes a slip from the hat and presses the written side against the seer's forehead. Just before the helper removes the slip and places it on the seer's lap, the seer asks the question and answers it. The seer is a little slower in answering the player's questions.

The seer makes up the first question himself. Thereafter he reads each slip as it is carefully laid on his lap, face upward. The other players, not knowing any questions but their own, do not suspect the trick in the first question and marvel at the seer's ability to "tell all."

Lucky Number

The leader asks the group members to stand and each selects any number between 1 and 100. He tells them to keep the same number and not to vary it. The leader selects a number (say 37). Then he might say, "If your number is below 25 or more than 75, sit down," and naturally a large portion of the group is eliminated. Next he might say, "If your number is not between 25 and 55, sit down," and still others are out of the game. Then, "If your number is between 36 and 40, remain standing. If you chose 37 or 38 remain standing." Lastly number 38 sits down. The lucky number is 37.

Magic Wand

The leader announces he has a magic wand and that it can find hidden objects. He asks the audience to produce something to be hidden. The leader then sends his accomplice from the room until the object has been hidden on one of the people lined up. The accomplice is called back and the leader places the wand lightly on the indicator, who may be another person from the audience or one of the nine people who does not have the hidden object, at one of the number spots that indicates to the accomplice which person in the line has the object.

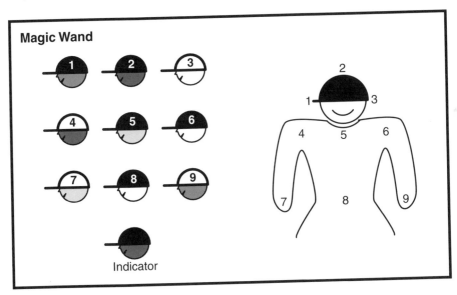

Magic Wand

Indicator

The accomplice takes the wand and walks past all of the others, trying to save the person who has the object until near the last. When he nears the person who has the object, he begins to vibrate the wand, and as he stands in front of that person, the wand vibrates wildly. He then announces who has the object.

Super Mind-Reading Stunt

The group selects a well-known person—fictional, living, or dead. The leader transmits the name to the accomplice by signals. All signals are seen or heard by the group, but few people can figure out the trick when they see it for the first time, or for that matter, for the tenth time!

In the first place, the actual name of the person selected is never transmitted unless there is no other way of informing the accomplice. The leader gives leads that are words associated with the selected name. It is up to the accomplice to put these words of association together and to figure out from them the identity of the person selected.

Suppose the person selected by the group is Marie Curie. The leader could give one word of association and the accomplice could guess that. *Radium* would do the trick. The word *radium* would be spelled out to the accomplice.

The spelling is done this way. The consonants are given by taking the accomplice "on a trip." The first letters of the cities mentioned are the consonants in the word being spelled. Thus, to spell *radium* the leader might start the trip at Rochester.

The vowels are given in a different way. This is always confusing to the listeners. The vowels are numbered as they appear in the alphabet—*A* is one; *E* is two; *I* is three; *O* is four; *U* is five. While taking a trip to Rochester we stop for *one* night. That gives the *A* in radium. From Rochester we go to Denver, giving the *D*. We stay in Denver *three* nights and *five* days, giving the *I* and *U*. We finish the trip in Memphis. This gives us the final *M*.

If the accomplice fails to guess, a new clue may be given. When more than one word is used, a change of method of transportation indicates the break between the words. For instance, the leader might say: "Let's take a train from there," or "We go by plane to Memphis."

The trick needs two fairly well-informed people to perform it as the groups often select persons hard to identify. An intellectual group of adults will find it exciting and challenging.

The Mysterious Cup

While the confederate is out of the room, a coin is placed beneath a cup. Upon returning, he touches the bottom of the cup and instantly tells the value of the coin unless it be gold, where upon he says, "Gold." The system of signaling is the direction in which the handle of the cup is pointing—one of seven positions as shown in the diagram.

Black Magic

The confederate leaves the room. Then anyone chooses something in the room. The leader brings back his confederate. The leader asks him a number of things and when he hits the right one he will say so. Here is how the game is played. The confederate will know what it is because just before the leader names the

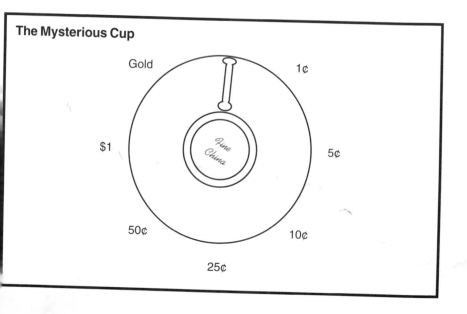

The Mysterious Cup

Gold   1¢

$1   *Fine China*   5¢

50¢   10¢

25¢

right one he will name something black and then the confederate knows the next thing the leader names is it.

Nope

Player A and player B know the "secret" for this game. Player A leaves the room while the group selects an object in the room. When he returns, player B points to an object that was not selected, asking, "Is this it?" Player A replies, "No." A second object not selected is pointed to, this time with the answer, "Nope." This is the signal that the right object should now be pointed out. Accordingly, player B points to it, asking the same question as before. Player A declares it to be the right one.

Crayon Mind Readings

A colored crayon is put in the hands of the mind reader behind his back. Still, after a deep thought, he is able to reveal the color of the crayon.

Solution:
The mind reader turns his back to the audience, and the crayon is placed into his right hand. He now faces the audience, reaches behind him with his left hand, and takes the crayon with this hand. He places his right hand on his forehead in a posture of deep thought, but he has scraped a little of the crayon onto his right thumbnail, as he glimpses this color when he places his hand on his forehead in deep concentration.

Mystery Game

One, two, or three players leave the room. The rest decide on something in the room; say, a safety pin, the cap of a bottle, somebody's shoe, anything but it must be in plain sight and something not too easy to guess.

Then the players sent from the room are called back and they try to guess what it is. They may ask questions of any type and as many as they wish which can be answered yes or no. They may ask any person they choose and all must answer truthfully.

Alphabet

The leader supplies the team with large cardboard letters, enough to form common words. One team secretly selects a word to spell. Letters to form the word are individually allotted to the various team members by the captain, and each person rushes to the preestablished team goal line, holding her letters over her head. The other team or teams are supposed to recognize and call out the word before it is formed. A team recognizing an unformed word wins one point. Any team failing to complete the word before an opponent calls it loses one point. The team with the highest score wins.

Variations:

- A variation may be for each team to have its letters jumbled on a table. The game leader calls a word. The team being able to spell out the word at its goal line with the single letters in the shortest time scores one point. Others sustain an equal loss.

Index of Games

^{BE}Games for the Beach; ^{MG}Games for the Middle Grades; ^{MY}Mystery Games; ^{PG}Games for the Primary Grades; ^{RR}More Relay Races; ^{SO}Games for Special Occasions; ^{UG}Games for the Upper Grades

Index of Games

[BE]Games for the Beach; [MG]Games for the Middle Grades; [MY]Mystery Games; [PG]Games for the Primary Grades; [RR]More Relay Races; [SO]Games for Special Occasions; [UG]Games for the Upper Grades

---

[BE]Games for the Beach; [MG]Games for the Middle Grades; [MY]Mystery Games; [PG]Games for the Primary Grades; [RR]More Relay Races; [SO]Games for Special Occasions; [UG]Games for the Upper Grades

Index of Games

[BE]Games for the Beach; [MG]Games for the Middle Grades; [MY]Mystery Games; [PG]Games for the Primary Grades; [RR]More Relay Races; [SO]Games for Special Occasions; [UG]Games for the Upper Grades

---

^(BE)Games for the Beach; ^(MG)Games for the Middle Grades; ^(MY)Mystery Games; ^(PG)Games for the Primary Grades; ^(RR)More Relay Races; ^(SO)Games for Special Occasions; ^(UG)Games for the Upper Grades

BEGames for the Beach; MGGames for the Middle Grades; MYMystery Games; PGGames
for the Primary Grades; RRMore Relay Races; SOGames for Special Occasions; UGGames
for the Upper Grades

[BE]Games for the Beach; [MG]Games for the Middle Grades; [MY]Mystery Games; [PG]Games for the Primary Grades; [RR]More Relay Races; [SO]Games for Special Occasions; [UG]Games for the Upper Grades

[BE]Games for the Beach; [MG]Games for the Middle Grades; [MY]Mystery Games; [PG]Games for the Primary Grades; [RR]More Relay Races; [SO]Games for Special Occasions; [UG]Games for the Upper Grades

Other Books From Venture Publishing, Inc.

The A•B•Cs of Behavior Change: Skills for Working With Behavior Problems in Nursing Homes
    by Margaret D. Cohn, Michael A. Smyer, and Ann L. Horgas
Activity Experiences and Programming Within Long-Term Care
    by Ted Tedrick and Elaine R. Green
The Activity Gourmet
    by Peggy Powers
Advanced Concepts for Geriatric Nursing Assistants
    by Carolyn A. McDonald
Adventure Programming
    edited by John C. Miles and Simon Priest
Aerobics of the Mind: Keeping the Mind Active in Aging—A New Perspective on Programming for Older Adults
    by Marge Engelman
Assessment: The Cornerstone of Activity Programs
    by Ruth Perschbacher
Behavior Modification in Therapeutic Recreation: An Introductory Manual
    by John Datillo and William D. Murphy
Benefits of Leisure
    edited by B. L. Driver, Perry J. Brown, and George L. Peterson
Benefits of Recreation Research Update
    by Judy M. Sefton and W. Kerry Mummery
Beyond Bingo: Innovative Programs for the New Senior
    by Sal Arrigo, Jr., Ann Lewis, and Hank Mattimore
Beyond Bingo 2: More Innovative Programs for the New Senior
    by Sal Arrigo, Jr.
Both Gains and Gaps: Feminist Perspectives on Women's Leisure
    by Karla Henderson, M. Deborah Bialeschki, Susan M. Shaw, and Valeria J. Freysinger
Dimensions of Choice: A Qualitative Approach to Recreation, Parks, and Leisure Research
    by Karla A. Henderson
Effective Management in Therapeutic Recreation Service
    by Gerald S. O'Morrow and Marcia Jean Carter
Evaluating Leisure Services: Making Enlightened Decisions
    by Karla A. Henderson with M. Deborah Bialeschki

Everything From A to Y: The Zest Is up to You! Older Adult Activities for Every Day of the Year
    by Nancy R. Cheshire and Martha L. Kenney

The Evolution of Leisure: Historical and Philosophical Perspectives (Second Printing)
    by Thomas Goodale and Geoffrey Godbey

Experience Marketing: Strategies for the New Millennium
    by Ellen L. O'Sullivan and Kathy J. Spangler

Facilitation Techniques in Therapeutic Recreation
    by John Dattilo

File o' Fun: A Recreation Planner for Games & Activities—Third Edition
    by Jane Harris Ericson and Diane Ruth Albright

The Game and Play Leader's Handbook: Facilitating Fun and Positive Interaction
    by Bill Michaelis and John M. O'Connell

The Game Finder—A Leader's Guide to Great Activities
    by Annette C. Moore

Getting People Involved in Life and Activities: Effective Motivating Techniques
    by Jeanne Adams

Great Special Events and Activities
    by Annie Morton, Angie Prosser, and Sue Spangler

Hands on! Children's Activities for Fairs, Festivals, and Special Events
    by Karen L. Ramey

Inclusive Leisure Services: Responding to the Rights of People With Disabilities
    by John Dattilo

Internships in Recreation and Leisure Services: A Practical Guide for Students (Second Edition)
    by Edward E. Seagle, Jr., Ralph W. Smith, and Lola M. Dalton

Interpretation of Cultural and Natural Resources
    by Douglas M. Knudson, Ted T. Cable, and Larry Beck

Intervention Activities for At-Risk Youth
    by Norma J. Stumbo

Introduction to Leisure Services—7th Edition
    by H. Douglas Sessoms and Karla A. Henderson

Introduction to Writing Goals and Objectives: A Manual for Recreation Therapy Students and Entry-Level Professionals
    by Suzanne Melcher

Leadership and Administration of Outdoor Pursuits, Second Edition
    by Phyllis Ford and James Blanchard

Leadership in Leisure Services: Making a Difference
    by Debra J. Jordan

Leisure and Leisure Services in the 21st Century
    by Geoffrey Godbey

The Leisure Diagnostic Battery: Users Manual and Sample Forms
    by Peter A. Witt and Gary Ellis

Leisure Education: A Manual of Activities and Resources
    by Norma J. Stumbo and Steven R. Thompson

Leisure Education II: More Activities and Resources
  by Norma J. Stumbo
Leisure Education III: More Goal-Oriented Activities
  by Norma J. Stumbo
Leisure Education IV: Activities for Individuals With Substance Addictions
  by Norma J. Stumbo
Leisure Education Program Planning: A Systematic Approach—Second Edition
  by John Dattilo
Leisure in Your Life: An Exploration—Fifth Edition
  by Geoffrey Godbey
Leisure Services in Canada: An Introduction—Second Edition
  by Mark S. Searle and Russell E. Brayley
Leisure Studies: Prospects for the Twenty-First Century
  edited by Edgar L. Jackson and Thomas L. Burton
The Lifestory Re-Play Circle: A Manual of Activities and Techniques
  by Rosilyn Wilder
Marketing for Parks, Recreation, and Leisure
  by Ellen L. O'Sullivan
Models of Change in Municipal Parks and Recreation: A Book of Innovative Case Studies
  edited by Mark E. Havitz
More Than a Game: A New Focus on Senior Activity Services
  by Brenda Corbett
Nature and the Human Spirit: Toward an Expanded Land Management Ethic
  edited by B. L. Driver, Daniel Dustin, Tony Baltic, Gary Elsner, and George Peterson
Outdoor Recreation Management: Theory and Application, Third Edition
  by Alan Jubenville and Ben Twight
Planning Parks for People, Second Edition
  by John Hultsman, Richard L. Cottrell, and Wendy Z. Hultsman
The Process of Recreation Programming Theory and Technique, Third Edition
  by Patricia Farrell and Herberta M. Lundegren
Programming for Parks, Recreation, and Leisure Services: A Servant Leadership Approach
  by Donald G. DeGraaf, Debra J. Jordan, and Kathy H. DeGraaf
Protocols for Recreation Therapy Programs
  edited by Jill Kelland, along with the Recreation Therapy Staff at Alberta Hospital Edmonton
Quality Management: Applications for Therapeutic Recreation
  edited by Bob Riley
A Recovery Workbook: The Road Back From Substance Abuse
  by April K. Neal and Michael J. Taleff
Recreation and Leisure: Issues in an Era of Change, Third Edition
  edited by Thomas Goodale and Peter A. Witt
Recreation Economic Decisions: Comparing Benefits and Costs (Second Edition)
  by John B. Loomis and Richard G. Walsh

Recreation for Older Adults: Individual and Group Activities
by Judith A. Elliott and Jerold E. Elliott
Recreation Programming and Activities for Older Adults
by Jerold E. Elliott and Judith A. Sorg-Elliott
Recreation Programs That Work for At-Risk Youth: The Challenge of Shaping the Future
by Peter A. Witt and John L. Crompton
Reference Manual for Writing Rehabilitation Therapy Treatment Plans
by Penny Hogberg and Mary Johnson
Research in Therapeutic Recreation: Concepts and Methods
edited by Marjorie J. Malkin and Christine Z. Howe
Simple Expressions: Creative and Therapeutic Arts for the Elderly in Long-Term Care Facilities
by Vicki Parsons
A Social History of Leisure Since 1600
by Gary Cross
A Social Psychology of Leisure
by Roger C. Mannell and Douglas A. Kleiber
Steps to Successful Programming: A Student Handbook to Accompany Programming for Parks, Recreation, and Leisure Services
by Donald G. DeGraaf, Debra J. Jordan, and Kathy H. DeGraaf
Therapeutic Activity Intervention With the Elderly: Foundations & Practices
by Barbara A. Hawkins, Marti E. May, and Nancy Brattain Rogers
Therapeutic Recreation: Cases and Exercises
by Barbara C. Wilhite and M. Jean Keller
Therapeutic Recreation in the Nursing Home
by Linda Buettner and Shelley L. Martin
Therapeutic Recreation Protocol for Treatment of Substance Addictions
by Rozanne W. Faulkner
A Training Manual for Americans With Disabilities Act Compliance in Parks and Recreation Settings
by Carol Stensrud

 Venture Publishing, Inc.
1999 Cato Avenue
State College, PA 16801

Phone: (814) 234-4561; Fax: (814) 234-1651